Curio
of the

British Library Cataloguing in Publication Data

Rodgers, Frank
 Curiosities of the Peak District and Derbyshire.
 1. Peak, Eng. - Description and travel - Views
 2. Derbyshire, Eng. - Description and travel - Views
 I. Title
 914.25'11'04850222   DA670.D43

 ISBN 0-903485-47-8

ISBN 0 903485 47 8

© Frank Rodgers 1979

2nd printing 1985

All rights reserved. No part of this publication may be reproduced, stored in a retrieval system, or transmitted in any form or by any means, electronic, mechanical, photocopying, recording or otherwise, without prior permission of Moorland Publishing Company Ltd.

Printed in the UK by Dotesios (Printers) Ltd, Bradford on Avon, Wilts for the publishers Moorland Publishing Co Ltd, Station Street, Ashbourne, Derbyshire, DE6 1DE England.

Frank Rodgers

Curiosities
of the Peak District and Derbyshire

Moorland Publishing

The numbers on this map refer to the curiosities in the contents list. Each feature also has a reference, eg C7, which enables its location to be found easily.

Contents

Introduction
1. Chesterfield's Twisted Spire E4
2. Naboth's Vineyard D4
3. An Ill-fated Queen D4
4. Bull i' th' Thorn B4
5. Sheepwash Bridge C4
6. Octagonal Church C3
7. Lullington Spud D11
8. Crypt at Repton D9
9. Cromford Canal E6
10. Cromford Mill D5
11. Cromford Bridge and Chapel D5
12. A Curious Inscription D5
13. Viator's Bridge C4
14. Charles Cotton's Fishing Temple B5
15. Ford Hall Dovecote E5
16. Bakewell's Icehouse C4
17. Halter Devil Chapel D7
18. Captured in Church C8
19. Derbyshire's Black Hole A3
20. The Plague at Eyam C3
21. Riley Graves C3
22. Mompesson's Well C3
23. Village Lock-up E10
24. Pinfold and Lock-up G8
25. Bull Rings C3
26. Village Stocks A3
27. House of Confinement F6
28. Alfreton O Miles! F6
29. Winster Market Hall D5
30. Riber Castle D5
31. Rowtor Rocks D5
32. Mock Beggars Hall C5
33. Cratcliffe Hermitage C5
34. Buxton Crescent A4
35. Victorian Letterbox A4
36. Ecton Copper Mines B5
37. 'Cathedral of the Peak' C3
38. Wayside Pulpit D3
39. Rock Basins D6
40. Wishing Stone D5
41. Derby Cathedral Tower E8
42. 'Our Lady of ye Brigge' E8
43. The Plague in Derby E8
44. 'Pece of Irron Worke' E8
45. A Converted Windmill E9
46. Cat and Fiddle Windmill F7
47. Toll Tablet F9
48. Canal Milepost F9
49. Church and House Combined F8
50. Dale Abbey Hermitage F8
51. Grave in a Field C5
52. Lost River C5
53. Elaborate Sundial C3
54. Early Sundial F8
55. Mystery Stone at Hopton D6
56. Ornate Barn D6
57. Revolution House E3
58. Chapel in a Field E4
59. Padley Chapel D3
60. Steetley Chapel G3
61. Crispin Inn E5
62. Lead Font E5
63. House of Cinders F7
64. Tufa Cottage D5
65. Horseshoe Bridge E9
66. Coldwall Bridge C6
67. Little John's Grave D3
68. A Veteran Yew Tree D5
69. Robin Hood's Picking Rods A1
70. Three Shire Heads A4
71. Dove Head A4
72. Goyt Bridge A4
73. Moot Hall D6
74. Odin Mine Crushing Mill B2
75. Wakebridge Engine House E6
76. Monsal Dale Viaduct C4
77. Peak Forest Tramway B3
78. Cromford and High Peak Railway D6
79. Middleton Top Engine House D6
80. Eldon Hole B3
81. Mam Tor B2
82. Nine Ladies D5
83. Cork Stone D5
84. Tower on Stanton Moor D5
85. Stanton Tower Doorway D5
86. Stanton Moor Carvings D5
87. Roman Pig of Lead E8
88. Roman Milestone A4
89. Roman Altar D4
90. Rock Chair D6
91. Roosdyche A3
92. Prehistoric Burial Chambers C6
93. Arbor Low C5
94. Melbourne 'Birdcage' E9
95. Melbourne 'Birdcage' Roof E9
96. Yew Tunnel E9
97. Cruck House E9
98. Anchor Church E9
99. Lud's Church A5
100. Eyam's Saxon Cross C3
101. Cross, Stile, Cross C6
102. Fine Wayside Cross B3
103. Lost Market Town D4
104. Lion's Head Rock C6
105. Fenny Bentley Hall C6

106	The Beresford Tomb	C6
107	Unfinished Millstones	D3
108	Trough on the Moors	D3
109	Toad's Mouth Rock	D3
110	Carl Wark	D2
111	Blue John	B2
112	Snake Pass	B1
113	Peak Cavern	C2
114	Rope Making in Peak Cavern	C2
115	Peveril Castle	C2
116	Haunted Highlow Hall	C3
117	Hazlebadge Hall	C3
118	Winnats	B2
119	Eagle Stone	D3
120	Tiny Guard House	D4
121	Unusual Clock Face	D4
122	Dog Whips in Church	D4
123	Bess of Hardwick's Monument	E8
124	Dorothy Vernon's Monument	C4
125	Swarkeston Bridge	E9
126	An Uncrowned King	F9
127	Balcony Field	E9
128	Early Iron Furnaces	E6
129	Crich Stand	E6
130	Tower on the Chevin	E7
131	Peter's Stone	C3
132	Little St Paul's	C7
133	Parson's Tor	C4
134	Nelson's Monument	D4
135	Victory, Defiant and Royal Soverin	D4
136	Wellington's Monument	D3
137	Moorland Guidestone	D3
138	England's Second Oldest Font?	F8
139	Stones from the Sea	F9
140	Remarkable Coffin Lid	D6
141	Joseph Sowter's Second Wife	E7
142	Norbury Tombchests	B7
143	A Wonderful Lectern	E8
144	Unusual Norman Font	C5
145	Derbyshire's Canal Pioneer	B3
146	Ironwater Spring	E8
147	Mermaid's Pool	A5
148	Winking Eye	A5
149	Lost Village	C2
150	Devotion of Tip	C1
151	Derwent Packhorse Bridge	C1
152	Well Dressing	C3
153	Shrovetide Football	C7
154	The River Manifold Disappears	B6
155	The River Manifold Reappears	B6
156	Congreve's Grotto	B6
157	St Bertram's Tomb	B6
158	Thor's Cave	B6
159	Railway in the Manifold Valley	B6
160	Manifold Dovecote	B6
161	Cottage Industry	E6
162	Relic of a Silk Mill	A4
163	England's First Silk Mill	E8

Introduction

This book originated from a series called 'County Curiosities' which ran for five years in the *Derbyshire Advertiser* and aroused great interest. It was frequently suggested that the series be published in book form, and in compiling this book of 'curiosities' the aim has been to make it as comprehensive as possible by including features, natural and otherwise, which arouse curiosity.

The area covered is of outstanding scenic beauty and includes the Peak District National Park, and it is hoped that the varied and fascinating features shown here will add to the appreciation of the Park, which an estimated 16 million people visit each year.

The rich variety of scenery in the Peak District and south Derbyshire stems from the extreme contrasts in its geological structure, from the alluvial deposits in the Trent Valley in the south, to the limestone dome of central Derbyshire and the gritstone moors in the north. It is on the limestone, which extends into Staffordshire, and the gritstone which also occurs in Staffordshire, Cheshire and Yorkshire and which together comprise the National Park, that so many natural features are found. It is on these windswept hills over 1,000 feet above the sea, that the elements have carved from the limestone deep gorges, honeycombing them with caves and sculpturing the white cliffs into strange shapes like the Lion's Head Rock in Dovedale. Through countless ages the hard gritstone of the moors has been worn away, leaving huge masses of harder rock weathered into realistic figures like Toad's Mouth Rock on Hathersage Moor, and Winking Eye on Ramshaw Rocks in Staffordshire.

Prehistoric man has left evidence of his habitation on the hills from the Neolithic period to the Iron Age, in the form of stone circles like Arbor Low, many burial mounds, and Iron Age forts like Carl Wark on Hathersage Moor. The Romans too left their mark on the landscape, a Roman altar and milestone having been found, and also Roman pigs of lead, indicating that they worked the hills for their minerals. There are extensive remains of later lead mining, copper mining, silk mills and cotton mills, pioneer work on canals and railways, all being studied as part of the subject of industrial archaeology.

The churches have many interesting features from Saxon, Norman and later periods, such as Repton's crypt, Youlgreave's font and the famous twisted spire of Chesterfield Church. Lesser known places like Halter Devil Chapel with its strange history, and curiosities like Anchor Church and Lud's Church with their legends are shown, together with other features connected with ghosts and superstitions. Memories of the plague and the happier events of ancient customs like well-dressing and shrovetide football are included.

Finally I would like to thank all those friendly people who never once refused my requests to take photographs, and also my friend Mr Roy Christian; Mr R.G. Hughes and Mr M.F. Stanley, for so kindly checking my manuscript.

1 Chesterfield's Twisted Spire   E4

The Devil, of course, is held responsible for the twist on Chesterfield's spire, although there are several different versions of how it came about. One says that a blacksmith at the nearby village of Barlow made a poor job of shoeing the Devil who, lashing out in agony as he passed over Chesterfield, gave the spire a violent kick. Another claims he was resting on the spire when a whiff of incense from below made him sneeze, and he had his tail wrapped tightly round the spire at the time! A more popular version in the town is that while resting there he twisted round in a bow to a beautiful and virtuous bride as she entered the church, but those born outside the county prefer the slanderous story that he jerked round in surprise because the bride was a virgin. Whichever legend you prefer, the twisted spire is world famous. Dating from the fifteenth century, it is 228ft tall and is not only twisted but also leans 7ft 6in to the south and as much to the south-west. It is generally thought that the twist was caused by the use of unseasoned timbers, with the weight of the lead plates which cover it.

2 Naboth's Vineyard   D4

This solitary cottage stands opposite the entrance to Edensor in Chatsworth Park, and is all that remains of the original village of about 1740. The Sixth Duke of Devonshire objected to the village being visible from Chatsworth House and had it demolished and rebuilt on its present site. This cottage remains because the owner is said to have refused to sell, and it became known as Naboth's Vineyard from the 1st Book of Kings, xxi. It is possible, however, that the occupant was very old, or a highly valued employee whom the Duke did not wish to disturb.

3 An Ill-Fated Queen   D4

Many long hours must have been spent by the unhappy Mary Queen of Scots in this raised summer house in Chatsworth Park. Queen Mary's Bower, as it is now called, dates from the first house built by Bess of Hardwick (see Plate 123), wife of Sir William Cavendish, who was her second husband. Her fourth husband, the Earl of Shrewsbury, was given the custody of Mary, who was at Chatsworth five times between 1570 and 1581. The moat which surrounds the bower is one of the fishponds of the old house and it is thought the structure may have been built specially for her, for her arms can be seen over the gateway at the top of the steps. High on the hill above stands the Hunting Tower, the only other feature remaining from the original Chatsworth House.

4 Bull i' th' Thorn   B4

As long ago as the thirteenth century the law demanded that a pole be projected from the wall of an alehouse to indicate that a new brew had been made so that the authorities could check it. As alehouses multiplied it was necessary for them to identify themselves, and what more convenient than the pole from which to hang a sign? The sun, moon and stars are common subjects on signs and probably among the first to appear. There are characters from folklore such as the Green Man at Ashbourne, and whimsical humour is shown in the Quiet Woman at Earl Sterndale (she has no head). Others are less easily explained, like the Bull i' th' Thorn, which stands beside the A515 Ashbourne to Buxton road about 5 miles south of Buxton, and claims to date from 1472. Carved in solid oak, the sign depicts a bull entangled in a thorn bush, a very effective way of depicting a possibly unique inn name.

5 Sheepwash Bridge   C4

Originally a packhorse bridge, Sheepwash Bridge at Ashford-in-the- Water has a curious addition which accounts for its name. The parapet has been continued to form an enclosure where sheep are still gathered to be driven out directly into the River Wye and across to the other side. Wheeled traffic has been banned from using the bridge in recent years in an effort to preserve it.

6 Octagonal Church   C3

Stony Middleton church is of a type unique in Derbyshire and rare elsewhere. The square tower is all that remains of the fifteenth-century church built by Joan Eyre as a grateful offering for the safe return of her husband from the Battle of Agincourt. The design of this church is unknown, but in 1759 this curious octagonal building was added to the tower. The interior is of interest, as all the pews face the centre. Near to the church are the so-called Roman Baths, a warm spring thought to have been known to the Romans. It is recorded that in 1777 these baths were nearly as hot as those at Buxton and were good for rheumatism. Today there is little to be seen except low buildings, now overgrown and in ruins, which were re-constructed by Lord Denman early in the nineteenth century.

7 Lullington Spud   D11

The church spire of Lullington, Derbyshire's most southerly village, is rather unusual and known locally as Lullington Spud. But a more curious feature is that although it has a clock, there are no clock faces. The clock is of an early type with no springs, and is driven instead by two stones weighing about 5cwt each. These are attached to ropes and wound up the tower each week, their weight providing the power as they are released slowly to the ground. A repair bill preserved in the church records that the clock was made by the village blacksmith over 200 years ago. The hours are struck on one of the bells, to give villagers and workers in the fields some idea of the time.

8 Crypt at Repton   D9

Repton is justly proud of its Saxon crypt beneath St Wystan Church. Kings and princes were buried here when Repton was the capital of the Kingdom of Mercia in the seventh century, a monastery having been built on the introduction of Christianity from Northumbria. When Wystan, a Saxon prince, was treacherously slain he was buried here, and the crypt became a shrine where miraculous cures were claimed to take place. In 875AD the Danes destroyed the monastery, but the crypt partly survived to be rebuilt, and the spiral pillars, unique in England, are thought to date from the tenth century. In 1172 a priory was built here which was destroyed at the Dissolution, and the crypt was forgotten until a gravedigger fell into it in the eighteenth century. Today this ancient place is claimed to be the most perfect example of Saxon architecture of its kind in England. Remains of the twelfth-century priory can be seen in the gateway of Repton School, and also in the lower parts of the guesthouse beyond, while the bases of huge pillars indicate the site of the priory church, for Repton School was built on the spot in 1556. The village cross on circular steps may have been the first spot in the Midlands where Christianity was preached.

9 Cromford Canal E6

One wonders how many travellers on the A6 Derby to Matlock road are aware of the historic canal which keeps them such close company between Ambergate and Cromford. Constructed 21 years after the death of Derbyshire's famous canal engineer James Brindley (see Plate 145), it was built by the railway pioneers Jessop and Outram. It was opened in 1793 to carry lead ore and stone from the Derbyshire hills, and no doubt it was a great day when the four stone lions, each 13ft long and fashioned in the Darley Dale quarries, were carried on the first stage of their journey to St George's Hall in Liverpool. The hall was also made from stone from Darley Dale; it was finished in 1854, the lions added a few years later. When the railway was built from Derby to Ambergate and on up the Amber Valley, gaily decorated boats carried Derby people from the train at Ambergate to see the sights of Matlock Bath. In 1849 the branch line to Matlock was built, squeezing its way between river, road and canal. The canal towpath can be joined at several points from the A6, and is one of the most delightful and easy five-mile walks in the county, passing through a tunnel and over river and rail. It links up with the High Peak Trail at High Peak Junction (see Plate 78), where the wharf and the beam engine used for raising water from the river have been restored by the Cromford Canal Society.

10 Cromford Mill D5

England's first water-powered cotton-spinning mill stands near the river bridge at Cromford. Built by Sir Richard Arkwright in 1771, it was powered by water from the Bonsall Brook and from a 'sough' draining the lead mines at Wirksworth (see Plate 73). The original building is now surrounded by later additions, the most striking being the one shown here, which was built in 1789 adjacent to the original and forming a new entrance. The sough which had helped to drive the mill was also used to feed the Cromford Canal, another venture in which Arkwright played a prominent part. Cromford is largely an Arkwright village, for it was he who secured a market charter and built the Greyhound Hotel. North Street and its school are other examples of his work, and by the river he built Willersley Castle and the church where he was buried.

11 Cromford Bridge and Chapel   D5

The ruined fifteenth-century bridge chapel at Cromford is an interesting survival from the days when travel was difficult and dangerous, and here thanks would be given for safe arrival and crossing the river. Swarkeston Bridge (Plate 125) also had a chapel, of which only the foundations remain, but that at St Mary's Bridge in Derby still stands (Plate 42). Close to the Cromford chapel is an eighteenth-century fishing temple similar to the one in Beresford Dale (Plate 14) and with the same inscription over the doorway. The original bridge, built for packhorses and contemporary with the chapel, has been widened with round arches on one side, the older ones down-river being pointed. The story is told of two artist friends who painted the bridge from opposite sides and quarrelled at home over who was right!

12 A Curious Inscription   D5

There is a cryptic inscription carved on the parapet of the bridge. This commemorates an amazing incident, the leaping of the parapet by a horse with a rider named Benjamin Haywood who lived at Bridge House nearby. Splashdown was successfully achieved in the river about 20ft below with the man still seated and neither hurt.

Another bridge inscription, at Ashford-in-the-Water, reads 'M Hyde 1664' but there the rider was thrown over the parapet into the river and was killed.

13 Viator's Bridge   C6

'What's here the sign of a bridge? Do you use to travel with wheel-barrows in this country?' So cries Viator in Charles Cotton's *Compleat Angler* (Part II) on approaching this bridge. Known now as Viator's Bridge, this tiny packhorse bridge crosses the Dove in Milldale, and we should note that the parapets have been added since those days, a fact which explains why Viator goes on to say that he would not ride over it for a thousand pounds ... 'yet I think I dare venture on foot, though if you were not by to laugh at me: I should do it on all fours.' Three miles upstream through Wolfscote Dale stands the Fishing Temple and one mile downstream through Dovedale the Lion's Head Rock (Plate 104).

14 Cotton's Fishing Temple   B5

The famous Fishing Temple stands on the Staffordshire bank of the Dove in Beresford Dale and is seen here from the footpath on the Derbyshire side, there being no longer any access to it on the other bank. It was built in 1674 by Charles Cotton (who lived at Beresford Hall, now demolished) for himself and his famous friend Isaak Walton, and over the doorway are their entwined initials with the words 'Piscatoribus Sacrum'. This building is still 'sacred to fishermen' all over the world, but is on private ground. In Pike Pool nearby stands a tall pinnacle of limestone. A footpath from the delightful village of Hartington leads down into Beresford Dale, to continue beside the Dove through Wolfscote Dale, Milldale and Dovedale, one of the loveliest dale walks in Britain.

15 Ford Hall Dovecote   E5

Two hundred years ago the keeping of pigeons was the prerogative of the well-to-do, for dovecotes were built solely for breeding for food. Pigeons were an important food source, for in the seventeenth century there were 26,000 dovecotes, housing from 500 to 10,000 birds each. The whole of the inner walls were lined with nest boxes, and pigeon pie would be a welcome change from frozen meat from the icehouse. The introduction of rootcrops for winter feeding of animals in the eighteenth century led to the dovecote's decline, and the general use of commercial foods in the nineteenth century made winter feeding easier, so the dovecote fell into disuse. The flooding of the Amber Valley by the Ogston reservoir has created a new beauty spot, and the dovecote shown here, all that remains of Ford Hall, stands close to the dam itself, while other examples of various designs may be seen at Melbourne Hall, Haddon Hall, Highlow Hall near Hathersage, Knowsley Cross near Longnor and Ridgeway Farm near Repton.

16 Bakewell's Icehouse   C4

Refrigeration is not new, for until a century ago most houses of importance had an icehouse for the storage of meat and other perishables. Before the introduction of turnips and swedes many cattle had to be slaughtered in the autumn, and the advantage of a large cold store can be appreciated. A circular pit lined with brick or stone and with a domed roof covered with earth was the usual type, but there are others. Alternate layers of meat and ice from the lake were laid within the pit, with straw as insulation. Within the hall ice boxes beneath the thrawls of huge kitchens were replenished with ice and meat from the ice house, and these great chests lined with zinc also held fish, wine and fruit. There are still a number of icehouses left in the county, but two, at Alfreton Hall and at Darley Abbey near Derby, have been demolished in recent years. Sometimes the icehouse was made into a landscape feature as in the case of this fine example on Castle Hill at Bakewell, where once stood an earthwork fortification built as a defence against the Danes. This

solid square building has a vaulted roof and is dated 1831 over its arched doorway. It originally stood in the grounds of Castle Hill House which was built in the late eighteenth century.

17 Halter Devil Chapel   D7

How this tiny chapel at Hulland Ward Intakes near Mugginton acquired the curious name of Halter Devil makes one of the strangest tales ever told, yet it seems substantially true. One dark and stormy night in 1723 a farmer, Francis Brown, decided to ride to Derby. He was very drunk, and met his wife's protests with the remark 'Ride I will, if I have to halter the Devil'. Fetching what he thought was his horse from the paddock, he was trying to put the halter over its head, with little success, when a flash of lightning had revealed that the animal had horns, and when Brown recovered, his conviction that it was the Devil was so great he became a sober man, and built this chapel adjoining his house. A stone tablet on the house wall was lost when the present house was built in 1873, but it carried the inscription:

Francis Brown in his old age
Did build him here a hermitage,
Who being old and full of evil
Once on a time haltered the Devil.

Although the chapel measures only 14ft by 13ft, a service is still held here in the afternoon of the last Sunday of each month, for on his death Brown endowed the chapel with 17 acres. It was never consecrated, being known simply by its strange soubriquet, but its founding and Brown's death in 1731 are recorded in Mugginton Church. The usual + indicates the chapel on the 1 inch ordnance map, about 1½ miles down the Mugginton road from Cross-o-th-Hands on the A517 Belper to Ashbourne road.

18 Captured in Church C5

In 1664, during the Civil War, 200 Royalist troops on their way to the relief of Wingfield Manor spent the night in Boylestone Church. Foolishly they had not placed guards, and in the early hours of the morning a small force of Roundheads quietly surrounded it. The cry to 'surrender or we fire' was made at all the windows and doors, and they were ordered to come out one by one through the narrow priest's doorway. To quote Sir John Gell, 'And soe wee tooke men, collours, and all, without losse of one man on either side.'

19 Derbyshire's Black Hole A3

A more terrible event of the Civil War than that at Boylestone was enacted in another Derbyshire church four years later. 1,500 Scottish prisoners taken at the Battle of Ribbleton Moor near Preston were locked in the church at Chapel-en-le-Frith for sixteen days. The church records show that when the doors were opened forty-four were dead, and many more died before the end of the long march back. The dead were buried in the churchyard but little remains of the church where they died. The original Chapel in the Forest was built here by the Keepers of the Royal Forest in the early thirteenth century, but the present church is mainly eighteenth century. Also worth seeing in the village are the sundials in the churchyard, the stocks in the Market Place, and the Hearse House just down the main street.

20 The Plague at Eyam   C3

The plague which ravaged London and spread over England in 1665, came to these cottages beside the church at Eyam in September, carried from London in a box of cloth. During the next 12 months the village lived in voluntary isolation, led by the Rector William Mompesson, and a Nonconformist Minster the Rev Thomas Stanley who had been turned out of the living there for nonconformity. By Christmas the death toll was forty-five, and by the end of the following year two-thirds of the population of 350 had died, among them Mompesson's wife Katherine, who had stayed with her husband after sending her children to safety. Her tomb lies in the churchyard close to the Saxon Cross, but people buried their own folk wherever was most convenient. In August a family named Hancock was afflicted, and within eight days the father and six children were, according to local legend, buried by the wife as best she could in the open field. Today they are grouped together under the care of the National Trust. During this time of self-imposed isolation help was organised by the Earls of Devonshire, food etc being left at agreed places at a safe distance and the money left in vinegar, a common practice no doubt insisted on by the people outside. There were several such places at Eyam. Today we know that vinegar has no value as a disinfectant, and it is also now suggested that the rigid isolation was not necessarily for the best. But all this took place in the unenlightened days of the seventeenth century, and we should not forget the fortitude of the people of Eyam, and the heroism of William Mompesson and Thomas Stanley. The plague at Eyam is commemorated in a service of memory held each year on the last Sunday of August, in a secluded little valley south of the village called the Delf. This is fitting, for it was here that Mompesson continued his services to a diminishing flock to reduce the risk of infection, preaching from a rocky outcrop since known as Cucklet Church.

21 Riley Graves   C3

The graves of the Hancock family, known as Riley Graves from the place name. A signpost on the Grindleford road just outside the village points the way and it is shown on the 1 inch ordnance map.

22 Mompesson's Well   C3

Named in memory of the devoted rector, this spring is one of the spots where food was left for the villagers. It lies on Sir William Hill on the left of the secondary Grindleford road about one mile outside the village. It is shown on the 1 inch ordnance map.

23 Village Lock-up   E10

'A night in the jug' is a term not heard much today, and would not be understood by many people if it were. Yet the 'jug' or lock-up can still be seen in our villages as a relic of a past way of life. Most of them date from the seventeenth and eighteenth centuries when, it is said, gin became cheap enough for working folk to afford. Drunks and minor lawbreakers were locked up by the village constable until they had cooled off, or while waiting escort to a court. Usually round or octagonal, the lock-ups had very small windows or none at all, and a heavy studded door. Derbyshire has two similar octagonal examples of brick, at Smisby and Ticknall, and circular types built of stone can be seen at Breedon just over the Leicestershire border, and at Alton in Staffordshire.

24 Pinfold and Lock-up   G8

Animals as well as people were often impounded in an enclosure specially built in the village. Stray animals were kept there until claimed on payment of a fine to the 'pinder'. Such a pound, or pinfold, can be seen combined with a lock-up opposite the Bluebell Inn at Sandiacre, a rather unusual yet quite logical arrangement. A plaque on the wall states 'Erected as a village lock-up, and pound for the imprisonment of stray animals about the year 1660AD.'

25 Bull Rings   C3

The barbaric 'sport' of bull-baiting was declared illegal in 1835, and at least four bull rings remain in Derbyshire, at Snitterton, Bonsall, Eyam and this one at Foolow. A tethered bull being set upon by dogs was a spectacle for the whole populace led by the local dignitaries, and it is to the credit of Bonsall that it gave up this pastime 24 years before it was made illegal. In the similar practice of bull-running the animal was let loose in the streets after being blinded and enraged by pepper, but this was enforced by law in the belief that it made the meat tender. In Chesterfield and elsewhere a fine of 3s 4d was incurred if the animal was not subject to running before being slaughtered in the Shambles.

26 Village Stocks   A3

Centuries ago you could have found yourself in the village stocks for drinking in the inn during the hours of church service, and you would have been put there by the churchwarden. You could also have been apprehended, sentenced and put in the stocks by the village constable for using foul language, gambling on Sunday, or even refusing to help with the harvest. There you would be the target for abuse and any filth anyone cared to throw. Sometimes a whipping post would be attached to the stocks, men and women being whipped bare-backed. The county has no whipping posts, but stocks remain at Eyam, Birchover, Sudbury and these at Chapel-en-le-Frith.

27 House of Confinement F6

Alfreton's lock-up, as befits the name 'House of Confinement' inscribed over the door, is a much more pretentious building than the usual round or octagonal types (see Plate 23). It was built for both sexes and has two rooms, each with a circular window, and dates from 1815. It stands near the bottom of the main street, the A61 Derby to Chesterfield road.

28 Alfreton 0 Miles! F6

This milepost, situated in the busy centre of Alfreton where the road to Mansfield branches from the A61 Derby-Chesterfield road, is usually passed unnoticed. Of a standard cast-iron pattern, it stands against the wall of the George Hotel facing down High Street and solemnly records Alfreton as 0 miles away! Another interesting milestone at Matlock Bath has a curious location, for it can be seen in the wall of the well-known fishpond beside the main road. Being set low down near the water, it is read with difficulty, but it is inscribed 'Chatsworth 10 Bakywell 10 Manchester 45' and the date 1801AD.

29 Winster Market Hall D5

Although old market halls are fairly common features in our towns and villages, Derbyshire is not so well endowed. The ancient lead-mining town of Winster, however, has a fine example standing in the middle of the main street. This is justly preserved, for in 1906 it was acquired by the National Trust, the first property in the county to be owned by them. The lower arches of stone are thought to be 500 years old, the upper portion of brick and stone having been rebuilt in 1905 using the old material. Unfortunately some of the arches have had to be filled in for strength. The main street and market hall indicate that the town was once much more important than it is today, and it was one of the centres of the lead-mining industry. Winster still enjoys its wakes, pancake racing and morris dancing. Another fine market hall is at Bakewell, where it houses the National Park Information Centre.

30 Riber Castle D5

Dominating on its hill above the Matlocks, Riber Castle is very much a part of the scene of this beautiful area. Sometimes known as 'Smedley's Folly', it was designed and built as a home by John Smedley, who transformed Matlock into a spa in the middle of the last century. It is said that it was impossible to give it a water supply. The cost of £60,000 when it was built in 1862, gives some indication of the success of his Hydro, which straddles the hillside of Matlock Bank, and is now the headquarters of Derbyshire County Council. After Smedley's death Riber Castle became a boys' school, also a food store during World War II, and it then stood empty before being opened to the public as a fauna reserve.

31 Rowtor Rocks   D5

This striking pile of gritstone towers behind the Druid Inn at Birchover, and here there are natural rock basins and a huge rocking stone which no longer rocks, thanks to a gang of youths who toppled it in 1799. Like Mock Beggars' Hall across the valley (see Plate 32), Rowtor Rocks were once thought to have Druidical connections. The Rev Thomas Eyre, who lived close by in the seventeenth century, converted these rocks into a retreat, with glorious views over the hills and dales. Here there are caves, rooms and alcoves, three armchairs and square sockets which may have held crosses, together with other features, all linked by steps, and all carved from the rock. Thomas Eyre also built Rowtor Chapel, now Rowtor Church, but this has been completely altered. It has wood carvings from an unknown source, and fragments of carved Norman stonework from a church recorded in 1300 at the top end of the village.

32 Mock Beggars' Hall   C5

Shown as Robin Hood's Stride on the 1 inch ordnance map, this curious pile of rocks stands across the valley from Rowtor Rocks shown above, and was once also thought to have Druidical connections. The two 'chimneys' which look so realistic in the dusk and have given the rocks the popular name Mock Beggars' Hall, are 18ft high and 22ft apart, and have been given the names Weasel and Inaccessible by rock climbers.

33 Cratcliffe Hermitage C5

Nearby the crag called Cratcliffe Tors towers over some small cottages, behind which a path leads up to a hermit's cave sheltered by an ancient yew. There is a crucifix carved on the wall, and a niche which probably held a small lamp. Thought to be about fourteenth century, this place may have been the home of hermits who through the centuries would have perhaps helped travellers on the Portway, one of Derbyshire's oldest trackways which passes between the tor and Robin Hood's Stride. In a field over the cliff top are the remains of a stone circle with six stones still standing. The stone circle and cave are also shown on the 1 inch ordnance map, and all three features can be reached from the Portway, now a footpath which climbs from the A524 Winster to Bakewell road in the valley.

34 Buxton Crescent A4

The famous Crescent at Buxton, completed in 1784 for the Fifth Duke of Devonshire with a view to developing the ancient spa, cost £120,000, traditionally paid for from the profits of his copper mines at Ecton in the Manifold Valley. John Carr was the architect, and it was built of local stone together with the fine domed stables behind, now the Devonshire Hospital. The position of the Crescent at the foot of the Slopes is believed to be due to a stubborn landowner who asked too much for the preferred imposing site on the hill top. St Anne's Well, one of the seven wonders of the Peak, faces the Crescent. St Anne's Chapel, which stood here until closed by Henry VIII, was hung with crutches and sticks left by cured pilgrims. Old Buxton Market Place stands on the hill top, and claims to be the highest market place above sea level in England. It still keeps the stump of its old cross.

35 Victorian Letterbox A4

Unique in Derbyshire, this hexagonal letterbox stands opposite the Opera House in Buxton, where it was erected in 1867, and is a delightful piece of Victoriana. This type is known as the Penfield after its designer J.W.Penfield, and is one of four designs in use from 1866 to 1879. Today there are 101 still in use, 55 of them in London. The rest are scattered over England and Wales, the nearest to Derbyshire being three in Manchester and one in Salford. It is of local interest that the circular type in almost universal use today was first made by the famous Derby firm of Andrew Handyside in 1870.

36 Ecton Copper Mines B5

At Ecton, 1,200ft above sea level and about one mile below Hulme End in the Manifold Valley, are the famous copper mines. It is not known when copper was first found here, but in the seventeenth century it was worked successfully by the Earl of Devonshire with the help of German miners, and later in the eighteenth century by the Fifth Duke of Devonshire. The main shaft was eventually nearly 1,400ft deep and was the deepest mine in Britain in the eighteenth century. There were even boats in use in the mine 200ft below the River Manifold. A huge underground water-wheel 32ft in diameter was installed to keep the mines drained. Before a stamping mill was installed, women and children were employed to crush the ore. Working on piecework, their pay ranged from 8d to 2d per day in 1769. The Fifth Duke developed the area, building a school, church and inn, but today little remains except a few stone cottages, and a large modern house called The Hillocks, built on a mine tip, or hillock, and seen on the left of the photograph. The mines closed towards the end of the nineteenth century, and all we can see of this once busy industrial centre are slight indications of buildings beside the river, including those of a cheese factory, railway

station and adit mines. On the hilltop there are many mine shafts, some unprotected, with remains of an engine house and horse gin circle. The defunct narrow-gauge railway route (see Plate 159), now a footpath running from Hulme End to Waterhouses, threads the valley alongside the river and road.

37 'Cathedral of the Peak' C3

Should you trace a finger round every nook and cranny on the inside wall of Tideswell Church, your finger would travel exactly one mile! So it used to be popularly said of this splendid church, to emphasise the grand scale on which it was built. Deservedly called the 'Cathedral of the Peak', it was built in the fourteenth century and took about 75 years to complete, although it is thought the Black Death may have interrupted the work. The font has had a curious and colourful career, for in 1824 it was 'regularly used by the workpeople to mix their colours in when beautifying the church with blue and mahogany paint'! Although it was common practice in medieval times to paint the interior of churches, this effort at Tideswell at a time when such paint was being cleaned off is rather surprising. Today there is no sign of this beautifying nor have the restorers been at work, and the church remains unspoiled. Among many interesting features are fine modern wood carvings by a local craftsman, Advent Hudstone, whose family still practise close by the Market Place. William Newton, a native of Tideswell and 'Minstrel of the Peak', is buried in the churchyard.

38 Wayside Pulpit D3

Where the road from Curbar climbs through the cleft at Curbar Edge, on several of the large flat stones which lie around are carved biblical references, cut about the end of the last century by Edwin Gregory, a mole catcher employed by the Duke of Devonshire. Edwin Gregory was also a local preacher, and it is said that he carved these messages after surviving a serious illness.

39 Rock Basins D6

The rock basins one sees on the moors were long thought to have been cut by man for collecting water, but are now firmly believed to be natural. Water collected in a small depression softened the rock, and in dry weather grit would swirl round with the wind, so eroding it deeper through the ages.

This one is on Black Rocks above Cromford, a wonderful viewpoint giving a wide panorama over the river gorge at Matlock Bath and the hills around. The High Peak Trail (see Plate 78 and 79) runs past the foot of the rocks, and nearby is a picnic spot and nature trail.

40 Wishing Stone D5

Should you wish to partake of the benefits of this huge block of Millstone Grit, you have simply to walk round it three times and any wish will be granted. Unusual natural features such as this were often ascribed to the Devil, or some superstitious belief given to them. This one lies on Lumside at Lumsdale near Matlock.

41 Derby Cathedral Tower E8

The tower of Derby Cathedral, dating from 1527, is rated as one of the finest examples of the Perpendicular style in England. Legend claims it was built at the expense of the town's young people, but benefactors and 'church ales' went a long way to meeting the cost. Several Derbyshire villages brewed 'church ales' specially for wakes week, the profits being subscribed towards the cost of the tower. Originally the Parish Church of All Saints, the church was elevated to a cathedral in 1927. Amazing acrobatics by itinerant performers were permitted on the tower in the eighteenth century, the most remarkable being when a man slid down a rope to St Mary's Gate, pulling a boy in a wheelbarrow. He was followed by an ass equipped with a wooden breastplate and each leg weighted! When the rope broke, bones were broken among the great crowd gathered to watch this crazy entertainment. There are over forty members of the Cavendish family interred beneath the church, and here is Bess of Hardwick's monument (Plate 123) and fine wrought-iron work by Robert Bakewell.

42 'Our Lady of ye Brigge' E8

The fourteenth century chapel on St Mary's Bridge is Derby's finest historical feature, and one of only five complete bridge chapels still standing in the country. It stands on the remains of the arches of the first stone bridge of 1326, now sandwiched between the present St Mary's Bridge of 1794 and the modern concrete span of Causey Bridge. On the original bridge curious tolls were charged, among them 'Salted eels paid 1p and 10 pigs paid 1d'. A trapdoor in the floor of the chapel gave access to the river, and there is a hole in the wall where dole was handed out to the poor in the street. It has been a store room and dwelling house, and in 1857 it was a carpenter's shop where woodwork for St Michael's Church was made. A grim episode took place on the bridge in 1588, the impaling of the dismembered bodies of the Padley Martyrs on spikes (see Plate 59). After many vicissitudes this tiny chapel,

measuring 45ft long by 14ft wide, is now preserved, purchased by the Derbyshire Archaeological Society and restored in 1930.

43 The Plague in Derby   E8

Derby suffered several times from the plague, perhaps the worst being in 1592 when 464 people died in the five central parishes. Farmers were afraid to trade in the town and grass grew in the Market Place. Famine was feared but averted when the farmers agreed to leave their produce at the Headless Cross on Nun's Green, north of the town. With tobacco in their mouths they returned later to collect the money from bowls filled with vinegar as a protection against infection. Thought to date from the fourteenth century, the cross had already lost its head by the fifteenth, being recorded then as the Hedles Cros or Broken Crosse, and it now stands in the Arboretum.

44 'Pece of Irron Worke'   E8

July ye 5 1718
Received of Mr Charles Banskin ye sum of twelve pounds in full for a pece if Irron Worke and Stone Worke done for ye font in Worbors Church.
I say received p me. £12.0.0 Robert Bakewell'
Some years ago this receipt was found at Radbourne Hall, and positively identified the wrought-iron font cover in St Werburgh's Church in Derby as the work of Robert Bakewell, Derby's fine eighteenth-century craftsman. It was found in the church cellar about 1894, broken and rusty. Examples of his work in Derby are the gates behind St Werburgh's Church, the Cathedral gates and screen and the Silk Mill gates in Wardwick.

45 A Converted Windmill E9

The ruined windmill on a hill near Melbourne has taken on a new role, for the renovated tower has been made into a lookout-tower for the Staunton Harold Reservoir. The road through the gateway is public, and continues up to the mill and a large car park, giving a splendid view of the new reservoir.

Other windmills, unfortunately in sadly ruinous condition, still stand at South Normanton, Carsington, Ashover and Fritchley, but those at Belper and Findern have been converted into unusual and attractive dwellings. The fine tower mill at Heage has been renovated by Derbyshire County Council.

46 Cat and Fiddle Windmill F7

The county's only complete windmill stands on the hill above Dale Abbey village (see Plates 49 and 50), and although no longer grinding corn, is still in perfect working order after 200 years. The whole wooden structure weighing about 50 tons revolves on a central post (the earliest type), being turned into the wind by pushing against a tailpole. In high winds ropes around posts and gears cranked by hand have to be used. Today the mill is in first-class condition thanks to the Stanton Ironworks who own and maintain it, and visitors are fascinated by the interior with its millstones and wooden gears still exactly as when last used.

47 Toll Tablet F9

The days when tolls were charged for the use of bridges and roads have almost gone, but there are still some reminders of the practice to be found. The toll house at Cavendish Bridge over the river Trent at Shardlow was demolished soon after the bridge was washed away in 1947, but the slate tablet with its list of charges was saved. Probably dating from 1777 when the bridge was built, it was re-erected by the County Councils of Derby and Leicester in 1960 beside the road on the Derbyshire side of the river. Cleaned up, its lettering is as good as new, and the list of charges is amusing. Chaise, chair, waggon or wain crossed for one or two shillings according to the number of wheels, foot passengers paid one penny, while soldiers and horned cattle were only charged ½d each.

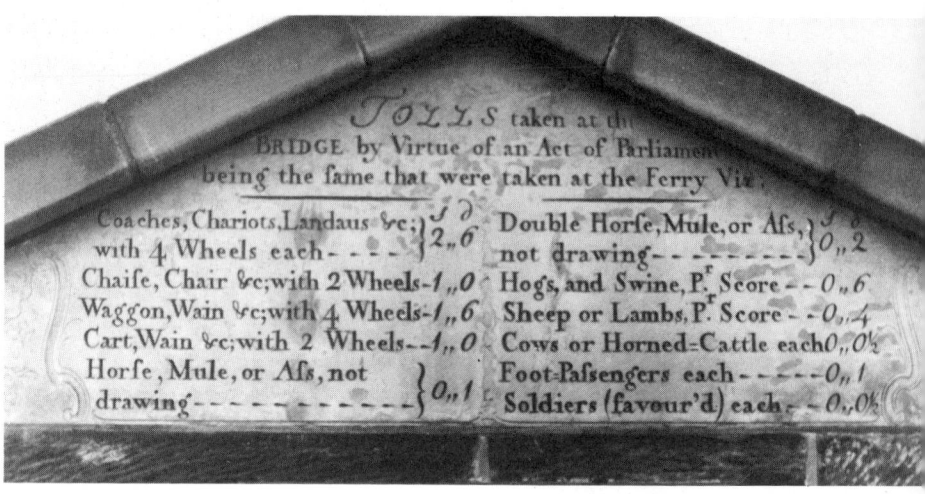

48 Canal Milepost F9

Ancient milestones can be fascinating (see Plates 28, 88 and 137), but one does not usually associate them with canals. This cast-iron milepost beside the Trent and Mersey Canal at Shardlow dates from 1819, although the canal was completed in 1777, and there are similar examples all the way to Preston Brook 92 miles away. Shardlow was an inland port long before this, when the Trent was navigable inland to Burton-on-Trent, and the canal brought further prosperity. Today Shardlow is a conservation area, and there are many interesting corners reminiscent of those busy days. The canal ends about a mile away at the confluence of the Derwent and Trent.

49 Church and House Combined F8

The church at Dale Abbey near Stanton-by-Dale shares its roof with a farmhouse which was once an inn called The Bluebell, and one could walk straight through for a drink after the service! Originally thatched, it dates from the twelfth century, and was built in memory of a hermit who had left his baker's shop in Derby after seeing a vision of the Virgin Mary. She had bade him go to Depedale where he lived in a cave upon the hillside. The Norman Lord of the estate, impressed by his sincerity, granted him tithes with which to build an oratory on the site of the present church. The interior is delightfully 'Walt Disney' with a balcony — approached by steps from outside — supported by posts all aslant, and a pulpit perched high in a corner. One can imagine it crowded with the Merry Men of Sherwood, for tradition says that here Alan a Dale was married, a distinction also claimed by Steetley Chapel (Plate 60). The huge east window of the Abbey nearby, built about 1160, is almost all that remains from the Dissolution.

50 Dale Abbey Hermitage F8

The Hermitage was probably a natural cave in the soft sandstone which has since been enlarged by man, and can be reached by following a short footpath behind the church. It lies in a wood on a steep hillside.

51 Grave in a Field C5

This grave, surrounded by railings and shaded by yew trees, is situated in a field not far from the road in Middleton-by-Youlgreave. Fittingly a stone cinerary urn surmounts the tomb, for here lies Thomas Bateman, a pioneer archaeologist whose name is well-known to those interested in the Peak District's prehistory. Bateman died in 1861 at the age of 39, and in his short life opened a great number of burial mounds and unearthed a vast amount of material now housed mainly in Western Park Museum in Sheffield. He lived at Lomberdale House just outside Middleton, and had the Congregational Chapel built in the village, choosing to be buried in an open field close by the chapel which has now been converted into a private dwelling. The field is private.

52 Lost River C5

Many Peakland rivers flow both above and below ground, sometimes leaving a dry course in summer, when the small amount of water sinks through the limestone to appear again lower down the valley (see Plate 154). About 100 years ago, however, the little River Bradford disappeared altogether for some years, astounding everybody by reappearing at Darley Dale where it joined the Derwent, having found its way underground for six miles. This was early in 1881, when heavy flooding swamped disused lead mines in the dale, which collapsed, revealing a hole 50ft wide and 20ft deep down which the river poured. Later debris and discoloured water emerged from a lead mine sough in Darley Dale which drained the mines around Alport, and the mystery was solved. Eventually the chasm was sealed and the Bradford resumed its normal course. A footpath follows the river from near Middleton-by-Youlgreave to its confluence with the Lathkill at Alport, a pleasant dale walk of just over two miles, with an ancient clapper bridge and a packhorse bridge near Youlgreave.

53 Elaborate Sundial C3

Of Derbyshire's many sundials, probably the most elaborate is that on Eyam Church. As well as the usual time of day, it gives the parallel of the sun's declination for the months of the year, the scale of the sun's meridian altitude, points of the compass, and a number of meridians together with the time in different parts of the world. This is amazing data for village folk of the eighteenth century, and one cannot help thinking it must be a copy, perhaps from Hampton Court, for its compilation would have been no mean task for the locals who are said to have made it in 1775. The Saxon Cross (Plate 100) stands close by.

54 Early Sundials F8

Our earliest surviving sundials, dating from Anglo-Saxon and Norman times, were very simple, consisting of lines inscribed on a stone with a peg for the stile or gnomon. A half circle indicated the period 6am to 6pm with four divisions to show the time for Mass (9am) and perhaps bell-ringing etc. Such a dial can be seen over the doorway of the church at Stanton-by-Dale and between these two extreme types there are many others to be seen in the county. Many of our large houses had their sundials, usually very ornate, to grace garden or house, but a more important secular use was in the market place. Trading times were strictly observed to give people living far and near an equal start, and many still remain on village cross or market hall, but Derbyshire has no such example.

55 Mystery Stone at Hopton D6

This carved stone is built into a cottage wall beside the road at Hopton near Carsington. The house dates from 1646 and possibly the stone was built in at that time, perhaps with others from the same source. St George and the Dragon may be discerned if one accepts a huge dragon and a tiny St George and horse; in fact the severed head of the dragon is larger than knight and horse. Assuming an ecclesiastical origin, it may have come from a demolished church now forgotten.

56 Ornate Barn D6

Not far from Hopton is a barn which seems to be of ecclesiastical design and is also of unknown origin. With carved mullion windows and an ornamental roof, it stands in a field about half way between Kirk Ireton and Bradbourne, and can be clearly seen from the road, from which it is reached by a footpath. It is of no particular architectural style, and it is thought that the ornamental stonework may have come from the same source as the Hopton stone, and been incorporated into the barn by a farmer.

57 Revolution House E3

A successful plot to overthrow the King was hatched in this pretty thatched inn at Whittington near Chesterfield in 1688. For three years James II, new to the throne, had encouraged Roman Catholicism contrary to law, leading to a plot by William Cavendish the Earl of Devonshire to overthrow him in favour of William of Orange. Here three noblemen met in what was then the Cock and Pynet (magpie), the outcome being the successful landing of William at Brixham in the same year. Once a busy little inn on the old road between Chesterfield and Sheffield, the building is now restored and open as a museum, with a sign telling how English history was changed here.

58 Chapel in a Field E4

The feelings of the people during James II's short reign were also manifest in events at the little Norman Chapel at Newbold, about two miles from Whittington. James had granted the chapel to the Catholics, but in the same year as the plot it was sacked by a Protestant mob. Measuring only 36ft by 18ft, it served as a barn for some years, but now it is preserved and stands curiously isolated in a field behind the Nags Head.

59 Padley Chapel D3

This building standing in a disused farmyard near Grindleford, was the private chapel of Padley Hall, the restored remains of which lie behind it. Here in the sixteenth century lived the Eyres, joined by marriage to the Fitzherberts of Norbury. Staunch Catholics, they came under the suspicious eye of Elizabeth, and in 1588 a raid led to the arrest of two priests, Nicholas Garlic and Robert Ludlam, who were hanged, drawn and quartered at Derby (see Plate 42). John Fitzherbert died in prison for harbouring them. The chapel became a cowshed to a farmyard, and was also used by the navvies who dug Totley Railway Tunnel, and at this time many of the carved timbers were burned. It was re-opened in 1933, and a pilgrimage is made here on the last Thursday in July in memory of the Padley Martyrs. To find the Chapel, one leaves the A6011 Sheffield road to Grindleford Station and Upper Padley is ¼m ahead.

60 Steetley Chapel G3

Tradition has it that Friar Tuck led Robin Hood and his Merry Men to prayer at this chapel near Worksop, and that Alan a Dale was married here. Prior to restoration in 1880 it had fallen sadly into decay, being used as a cowshed and lacking a roof for a long time. Today it is regarded as the finest example of Norman architecture in the county, but the reason why such a beautifully decorated little chapel — it measures only 52ft by 15ft — should be built here is unknown.

61 Crispin Inn E5

This old inn standing beside the churchyard gate at Ashover is famous, and a large colourful board on its wall records a little of its history. 'This house', it states, 'probably dates from the year 1416 when Thomas Babington of Dethick and several men of Ashover returned from the Battle of Agincourt, which was on St Crispin's Day. . . . In 1646 Job Wall, Landlord of the Inn, withstood the troops in the doorway and told them they should have no more drink in his house as they had too much already, but they turned him out and set watch at the door while the ale was drunk or wasted.' The troops were Royalist soldiers quartered nearby to cover the Matlock to Chesterfield road. There is another Crispin Inn at Litton near Tideswell, and among other famous inns should be mentioned the Newhaven Hotel on the Ashbourne to Buxton road, which has a perpetual licence free from the whims of licensing justices, granted by a satisfied George IV; the Peacock at Osgathorpe claimed as one of the stopping places of Dick Turpin; and the delightful Peacock at Rowsley.

62 Lead Font E5

As there are nearly forty lead fonts in England, it is rather strange that the Peak District, famous for its lead mining, should have only one. It is fitting that it should be at Ashover, which was an important lead-mining centre. The font is thought to date from 1150, and is about 2ft across and decorated with twenty figures about 8in high standing in arches around the sides. When the Roundheads came to Ashover they destroyed Eastwood Old Hall, the remains of which stand about one mile south-east, held a service in the church and then destroyed stained glass and records.

Almost certainly this font would have gone too, were it not for the vicar who had the foresight to bury it in his garden.

63 House of Cinders F7

Cinder House near Ilkeston is built of cinders and might be unique in England. The cinders are not from coal, however, but are specially prepared large pieces of clay burnt a rusty brown. The walls are 30in thick, and as the cinders are porous the house is warm in winter yet cool in summer. Originally built as two cottages by Francis Newdigate as an experiment in new materials, and to commemorate the birth of a son, it has the initials FN and date 1833 in red cinders over a window. The house is such a curiosity that Americans have tried to buy it, and the end wall facing the road has been reduced somewhat in thickness by souvenir hunters.

64 Tufa Cottage D5

This old keeper's cottage stands about half way along the Via Gellia, and is built of a porous stone called tufa, large quantities of which lay around this area. It is formed of calcium carbonate, deposited by water onto moss and solidifying, a process which continued as more moss grew on the new rock. The decay of the moss accounts for the spongy structure of the stone. A wide variety of objects 'petrified' with a coating of calcium carbonate deposited on them by water sprays, can be seen in the Petrifying Well at Matlock Bath.

65 Horseshoe Bridge   E9

This curious little bridge at Ticknall near Melbourne is in fact a railway bridge dating from about 1800, when this pleasant and peaceful village was very busy making bricks and pottery. The railway or tramway was narrow gauge with cast-iron rails fixed to stone sleepers, and continued from the bridge to pass through a small tunnel about 130yd long under the drive of Caulke Abbey. Its grass-grown track runs through cuttings and woods to Ashby four miles away, where it joined the main line. Its route is still shown on the 1 inch ordnance map.

66 Coldwall Bridge   C6

One of the county's 'lost' bridges, Coldwall spans the River Dove near Thorpe, south of Dovedale. It was built in 1762 to carry the road which linked the Blythe Marsh turnpike with the Ashbourne-Buxton road via Cheadle and Oakamoor. Today this small portion where it crosses the Dove Valley is still green; this pleasant spot with an old milestone of 1822 can be found by following the road past the church in Thorpe village.

67 Little John's Grave   D3

The reputed grave of Robin Hood's trusty giant Little John can be seen in Hathersage Churchyard. It is 10ft long and many years ago a 30in thigh bone was unearthed which seemed to indicate a man 8ft tall. The village claims that Little John lived there, and certainly a cap and bow firmly believed to be his hung in the church porch in the seventeenth century. The centre stone records that the grave is under the care of the Ancient Order of Foresters.

68 A Veteran Yew Tree   D5

The famous yew tree in Darley Dale Churchyard has grown younger through the years, for it was once firmly believed to be 2,000 years old but it is now thought to be less than 1,000 years. 33ft in girth, it is one of the largest in England, and has many visitors whose curiosity is aroused by the tablets erected round its base. These commemorate some of the outstanding actions fought in World War II. They were erected soon after each action took place, and are an interesting modern addition to the historic events sometimes recorded in churchyards through the centuries.

69 Robin Hood's Picking Rods   A1

The Peak District has its share of Robin Hood features, as it should, for Sherwood Forest is only just over the border. However, if all the features which bear his name in this county and beyond were genuine, his age would be as legendary as he himself was. His reputed grave is at Kirklees Priory in Yorkshire and there is Little John's grave at Hathersage. No one knows when Robin Hood's Stoup on Offerton Moor were first so named, nor the two wells bearing the names of Robin Hood and Little John near Longshaw Lodge above Hathersage. They are all shown on the 1 inch ordnance map. Robin Hood's Stride (Plate 32) indicates a mythical figure, but two round pillars set in a block of stone on Ludworth Moor near the Cheshire border near Glossop may have had a practical origin. Once known as the Maiden Stones, they are shown on the 1 inch ordnance map as Robin Hood's Picking Rods, and it has been suggested they were used for bending bows while stringing them. Certainly such a device would have made the task much easier. Other theories such as boundary stones or wayside crosses seem to be discounted as there are two stones and they are socketted into the base, indicating there always were two. Whatever their origin, these stones remain a mystery. This curiosity is situated about three miles south west of Glossop, standing beside a footpath which crosses Cown Edge from Monk's Road to a minor road which drops down into Chisworth. Basingwerk Abbey in Flintshire once owned land here, and what is thought to be the base of a cross called Abbot's Chair lies beside Monk's Road. Perhaps the Picking Rods have some connection with the monks' occupation of the area.

70 Three Shire Heads A4

At this lovely spot in the Dane Valley the counties of Derbyshire, Staffordshire and Cheshire meet at Pannier's Pool Bridge, which, as the name shows, is a packhorse bridge. There are several interesting tales concerning this lonely spot. It is thought that a court was held here in the fourteenth century, the business being trespassing in the nearby Forest of Macclesfield. It was held by order of the Black Prince, Lord of the Forest, the order reading, 'Tenants of the counties of Derby and Stafford who are indicted of trespass in the said forest — found guilty of such trespass shall give satisfaction as reason demands, while those not found guilty shall go free without let or hindrance — By command of the prince himself at Westminster, in presence of Wegefeld Stafford and Delves'. Many years ago gypsies settled in this spot for the winters, making counterfeit money to distribute in their travels. Whenever the authorities got wind of their activities it was quite easy for them to cross the streams into another county and avoid arrest. The name 'flash' for spurious money is said to come from the nearby village of Flash, which, incidentally, claims the highest church above sea level in England. There are several pleasant walks to the bridge, but be well shod in wet weather. A sign on the A53 Leek to Buxton road points to Knotbury, and from here a rough track leads down to the bridge. An easier approach is made from the A54 Buxton to Congleton road where a narrow road is taken to Knar and then a track on the left. Four packhorse tracks converge on the bridge, and it is interesting to observe that it has been widened, indicating the extensive traffic it once carried.

71 Dove Head A4

1,000ft above sea level on the flanks of Axe Edge the rivers Dove, Manifold, Dane and Goyt all have their beginnings, dividing Derbyshire, Staffordshire and Cheshire. Lovers of Dovedale may like to find the source of the Dove at Axe Edge End on the A53 Leek to Buxton road. From a stile opposite a farm a short path leads down to the spring which is shown on the 1 inch ordnance map. The stone covering bears the initials of Charles Cotton and Isaac Walton, but the inscription is of much later date. The Dove forms the boundary with Staffordshire for all of its length, and ends a romantic journey at its confluence with the Trent at Newton Solney near Repton.

72 Goyt Bridge A4

This 300-year-old packhorse bridge formerly stood at Goyt Bridge in the Goyt Valley, but due to the construction of a reservoir has, like that at Slippery Stones (Plate 151), been erected on a new site. Many tons of salt have crossed this bridge in the panniers of packhorses bound south and east along the old saltway from Cheshire. The reservoir owners, the Stockport and District Water Board, have paid for its re-erection higher up the valley about two miles from the A537 Buxton to Macclesfield road.

73 Moot Hall D6

Mental pictures of gold-mining in the frozen Yukon may be conjured up by the names of old mines such as Goodluck, Dream, Danger and Adventure, yet these and many more were given to the lead mines worked in the Peak hills. They were indicative of the hopes and despairs which went with the perilous business of finding, digging and smelting ore. The Romans worked the hills for lead (see Plate 87) and perhaps the Danes did also, and in the Middle Ages lead was in great demand for roofing, cisterns and churches. Prior to the Danish invasion the mines at Wirksworth were owned by Repton Abbey, the rent being paid in lead. When the abbey was destroyed by the Danes in AD875, the mines became the property of the Danish King, the area becoming the 'King's Field'. In 1288 the 'ancient custom of the mine' was settled at Ashbourne as a code of conduct, thus putting on record the old rules hitherto based on custom.

Wirksworth was for centuries one of the important centres for lead mining, and here lead mining disputes are still settled at the Moot Hall of 1814. Inside is preserved the bronze Miners' Standard Dish, the only one in existence, which was used for measuring the ore, as a levy had to be paid to the King, also a fee to the Barmaster for all lead mined. It dates from 1513. On the front of the hall carved tablets depict the various tools used.

74 Odin Mine Crushing Mill B2

An interesting relic of the lead industry is the remains of a crushing mill beside the road below Mam Tor, which served the Odin Mine, which may have been worked by the Danes. Odin Mine was first recorded in 1280 making it the oldest named lead mine in Derbyshire, although the crusher dates from 1823. Other features of this ancient industry are the remains of smelting mills such as those at Stone Edge above Ashover and those below Alport, and also the many 'soughs' or tunnels cut to drain the mines to the nearest river.

75 Wakebridge Engine House   E6

Evidence of this ancient industry lies all over the Low Peak in the form of deep scars gouged across hill and dale where a vein has been followed, shown on the map as 'rakes'. Hundreds of vertical shafts, not always protected by a 'beehive' of stones, dot the hilltops, while levels burrow into the hillsides. In all cases great care should be taken, for the shafts may be very deep and often flooded, while the levels sometimes contain shafts to lower levels. Timber supports may be rotten, and one should never venture inside. The larger mines had steam pumping engines, and engine houses can be seen at New Engine Mine above Eyam, and at Wakebridge below Crich Stand where two deep shafts are safely protected by iron railings. The mine buildings at Magpie Mine at Sheldon are used as a field centre by the Peak District Mines Historical Society, and there is now a permanent lead mining museum in the Pavilion at Matlock Bath.

76 Monsal Dale Viaduct   C4

'The valley is gone — and now every fool in Buxton can be in Bakewell in half an hour and every fool at Bakewell in Buxton, which you think a lucrative process of exchange, you fools everywhere.' So spake John Ruskin over the building of the railway viaduct in Monsal Dale in 1861, and in fact a photograph taken at the time does show the dale to have been a very sorry sight. Today the line is closed, but there are moves to re-open the portion between Matlock and Buxton as a conservation and tourist attraction. One day it is hoped once again to run trains along one of the loveliest stretches of line in Britain.

77 Peak Forest Tramway B3

Sixty-six years before the railway came to Monsal Dale, a tramway was built to extend the Peak Forest Canal at Buxworth (or Bugsworth as it was then known) to the Buxton area. Before the days of steam the waggons were horse-drawn, and on the steep inclines heavily loaded waggons were released to raise the others. Sleepers were of stone, as seen in this photograph on the incline into Barmough Clough. The line ran until 1915, and a wheel and small portion of flanged rail can be seen in Buxton Museum.

78 Cromford and High Peak Railway D6

An interesting aspect of this railway which threads the hills of the Lower Peak is the fact that it was built as part of the canal system. One of the earliest railways in Britain, it was constructed between 1825 and 1830 to connect the Cromford Canal (see Plate 9) in the Derwent Valley with the Peak Forest Canal in the Goyt Valley. The limestone plateau over which it passes rises to 1,000ft, making a canal impossible and a railway very difficult. Here is seen Sheep Pastures Incline where it climbs from the Cromford Canal to pass under the A6 Derby-Matlock road between Whatstandwell and Cromford. The gradient of 1 in 9 was worked by cable from an engine house at the top, with empty waggons helping to balance full ones. The curve of the lines enclosed a 'catch pit' into which the waggons fell if there was a fault, this being built after runaway waggons had leapt the road, canal and railway below. Where the A515 Ashbourne to Buxton road crosses the railway a plaque on the bridge gives the name of the engineer, Josias Jessop. This 33-mile-long railway has been stripped of its rails and is now the High Peak Trail, linking with the old Ashbourne to Buxton line at Parsley Hay which is now the Tissington Trail.

79 Middleton Top Engine House D6

A second incline, Middleton Incline near Wirksworth, has had its engine house at Middleton Top restored to working order and may be inspected at certain times. Here one may hire bicycles, as one may also do at Parsley Hay Station. These two trails thread sinuous routes over the limestone hills of central Derbyshire, and may be joined at many points by road and footpath.

80 Eldon Hole B3

A spectacle of awe and fear in the superstitious days of long ago, when it was thought to be bottomless, this pothole on the slopes of Eldon Hill is still a frightening place to many people. In the early part of the eighteenth century Daniel Defoe tells of a rope being lowered nearly a mile into Eldon Hole, but as we now know it to be 245ft deep, we can smile at the thought of the great mound of rope growing at the bottom. He also records the murder of a traveller who was forced to the edge by two villains until he 'stept at once into eternity'. In 1780 the hole was explored, revealing that a great mound of stones at the bottom sloped steeply for over 60ft into a huge cavern, its domed roof encrusted with stalactites. This pothole is the largest in Derbyshire, measuring 110ft long by 20ft wide, and one is advised not to climb the fence which surrounds it. Eldon Hole is one of the 'seven wonders of the Peak', the others being Mam Tor, Peak Cavern, Poole's Cavern and St Anne's Well at Buxton, Chatsworth House and the ebbing and flowing well in Barmough Clough which has unfortunately run dry.

81 Mam Tor B2

One of the outstanding features of the Peak, Mam Tor dominates the head of the Hope Valley near Castleton. Composed of alternate layers of sandstone and shale, the exposed side to the east is particularly susceptible to weathering, causing landslides which have sometimes swept away the road below. It is sometimes known as Shivering Mountain, and it was once popularly believed that its shadow never grew less despite the erosion of its side. The name Mam Tor is thought to derive from the Celtic, meaning 'mother mountain', and round its summit are the remains of the ramparts of a hill fort of the Iron Age. A road passes through Mam Nick on the side of Mam Tor, and a footpath leads to the top, 1,700ft above sea level, with wonderful views across Edale to Kinder Scout and the surrounding hills. The path continues along the ridge to Win Hill and so down to Hope, a fine walk. On the opposite side of the road to Mam Tor can be seen the famous Blue John Mine (Plate 111), and the Odin Mine crushing mill (Plate 74) can be found on the opposite side of the road to the mine where the road skirts Treak Cliff on its way to Castleton.

82 Nine Ladies D5

The Nine Ladies stone circle is the best known of the many prehistoric remains on Stanton Moor above Darley Dale, and is scheduled as an ancient monument. Thirty-three feet in diameter, its purpose is unknown, but much evidence of Middle Bronze Age people has been unearthed on the moor, and it is thought that here the religious and public functions of the tribe took place. About 100ft away is the King Stone, a pointer often found with such circles, which gives some credence to the theory that they were also used for astronomical purposes. These Middle Bronze Age folk cremated their dead, and over sixty burial mounds have been discovered, often containing cinerary urns and flint tools. The barrows were excavated under the direction of two local archaeologists, the late J.C.Heathcote and his son J.P.Heathcote,FSA, and much of the material found is in a private museum at Birchover nearby.

83 Cork Stone D5

Modern quarrying and stone cutting takes place on the south-western edge of Stanton Moor, and old overgrown quarries on the eastern side still have remains of the old craft, including millstones etc. A number of huge blocks of gritstone with names like Cork Stone, Cat Stone and Andle Stone lie around the moor, and these were long thought to have connections with early man. Today they are known to be natural features, harder stone left as the plateau wore down through the ages.

84/5 Tower on Stanton Moor   D5

Travellers through Darley Dale might notice the tower set high on the edge of the moor. This was erected as a tribute to Earl Grey who carried the Reform Bill through parliament, and over the door is inscribed his name and the date 1832.

86 Stanton Moor Carvings   D5

It is interesting to look for other carvings on the rocks around Stanton Moor. One is expertly and deeply cut in relief depicting a coronet over a Y with the date 1826. This commemorates the famous Duke of York. All are the work and tributes of the Thornhill family whose home, Stanton Hall, lies over the other side of the moor. From this eastern edge of Stanton Moor can be seen extensive views up and down the Derwent Valley. Over 27 acres, extending for three-quarters of a mile, are owned by the National Trust, given by Mr F.A.Holmes of Buxton in 1934.

87 Roman Pig of Lead   E8

Bearing the name of the Emperor Hadrian, who reigned in the early part of the 2nd century AD, this is a faithful copy of one of several lead pigs found in the Matlock-Wirksworth area, and is shown with a modern pig from the Millclose Mine in Darley Dale. The Romans, here from the first century to the early part of the fifth, attached great importance to the lead in the Derbyshire hills. Their roads criss-crossed the county from camps at Derby, Buxton, Glossop and Brough, and others entered the county from various directions. Of these camps little remains, although inscribed stones, coins and pottery have been unearthed. The foundations of Doctor's Gate which ran from Melandra at Glossop to Navio at Brough can still be seen where it climbs over Coldharbour Moor to cross the Snake Road. (Photo: courtesy of Derby Museum).

88 Roman Milestone   A4

The milestone, now in Buxton Museum, was found in 1856 on the east side of Buxton, and records that Navio is 11 miles distant along Bathamgate which ran between Buxton and Brough, and is the only one found in the county. (Photo: courtesy of Buxton Museum).

89 Roman Altar   D4

The altar dedicated to the god Mars, was found near Bakewell and is now in Haddon Hall. Translated it reads: 'To the god Mars Braciaca, Quintus Sittius Caecilianus, Praefect of the first cohort of Aquitani, performs his vow'. (Photo: courtesy of Haddon Hall Estates).

90 Rock Chair D6

Besides the natural rock formation which bear resemblances to various creatures like Lion's Head Rock (Plate 104) and Toad's Mouth Rock (Plate 109), there are others which definitely show the hand of man. Harborough Rocks is a great limestone outcrop near Brassington, and hereabouts lie several stones representing a font, pulpit and the chair shown here, which is very unlikely to be entirely natural. From a large cave here have been excavated objects from the late Palaeolithic to Medieval times, together with the bones of animals now extinct in these islands. Many Peakland caves were inhabited until a few hundred years ago, but there is no evidence to show when this chair was cut. At the foot of the rocks run the High Peak Trail, and there is a footpath to the road not far away giving easy access to the summit.

91 Roosdyche A3

This amazing valley on a hilltop east of Whaley Bridge has excited speculation for many years, for it has all the appearances of being artificial. Nearly three-quarters of a mile long and 40yd wide with sides up to 30ft high, this flat bottomed valley was for many years thought to have been a Roman race-course, a theory now completely discarded. Today the Roosdyche, as it is shown on the 1 inch ordnance map, is considered to be a glacial drainage channel, and is surely one of the Peak District's strangest freaks of nature.

92 Prehistoric Burial Chambers C6

It is amazing to realise that when the Roman soldiers were marching over Minninglow Hill, along their road from *Derventio* (Derby) to *Aquae Arnemetiae* (Buxton), these graves on the hilltop a short distance away had been here for 2,000 years. The five burial chambers of Neolithic man which crown this hill near Aldwark are thought to be of about the same period as Arbor Low, and are perhaps the best known in the Peak District. Here we see the actual chambers formed of blocks of limestone with a large covering slab. Such tombs were used for communal burials, for several skeletons were found in similar graves at Five Wells near Taddington. Many 'lows' or tumuli dot the hill tops in the Peak District and south Derbyshire and can be traced in numerous place names. The great majority of these are slightly later than the above, dating from the Bronze Age. Minninglow Hill is capped by a group of wind-swept beeches and on the southern slopes not far away runs the High Peak Trail (see Plate 78). The Roman road and tumuli are shown on the 1 inch ordnance map, but there is no public access to them.

93 Arbor Low C5

This mysterious 'henge' monument, often referred to as the 'Stonehenge of the Midlands', is the county's chief prehistoric monument. It stands 1,230ft above sea level on the limestone plateau of central Derbyshire, and is still the subject of speculation about its origin and purpose. Close by ran an important prehistoric trackway which also passed Minninglow to the south, and the Bull Ring at Doveholes north of Buxton, another 'henge' monument of which not a stone remains. Arbor Low is considered to have been a sacred place where religious rites were held. In 1901-2 the excavation of a male skeleton, without the usual goods which would normally accompany a man into the next world, might indicate a sacrifice. The circle of over forty stones, the largest of which is about 13ft long, point towards a small group in the centre, and are thought to have probably once stood upright. They lie on a circular platform about 160ft diameter, surrounded by a ditch and bank through which two entrances are cut to the north and south. It is thought to date from the early Bronze or late Neolithic Age, and is thus nearly 4,000 years old. There are many burial grounds clustered round the monument, and a later Bronze Age barrow built into the bank near the southern entrance has been excavated, and food vessels and cremations found. Similar items were found when Gib Hill, the county's largest tumulus which is situated about 350yd away, was partly excavated in 1848, and close beside it are the remains of what is thought to be a smaller and even earlier 'henge' than Arbor Low. Gib Hill and Arbor Low are both shown on the 1 inch ordnance map about one mile from the A515 Ashbourne to Buxton road near Parsley Hay.

94 Melbourne 'Birdcage' E9

Splendid in vivid colours, this wrought-iron summer-house stands in the grounds of Melbourne Hall. Popularly known as the Birdcage, it dates from about 1705, and is one of the finest examples of the work of Robert Bakewell. Little is known of this Derby craftsman except that he was poor at this time, needing advance payments to purchase the iron for this piece of work. The fashion of enhancing gardens and houses with artistic ironwork led to many orders, and further examples of Bakewell's work can be seen at Derby (Plate 44), Etwall, Tissington and Longford Hall gates, and Foremark Church altar rails and the gate in the churchyard. Other examples just outside the county are the gates at Okeover Hall (Staffs) near Mappleton, and the screen of Staunton Harold Church just over the Leicestershire border near Melbourne.

95 Melbourne 'Birdcage' Roof E9

96 Yew Tree Tunnel   E9

Another interesting feature of Melbourne Hall grounds is the curious yew tunnel, over 100yd long thought to have been planted in Charles I's time. That it was intended as a tunnel and not just an avenue, is proved by a record of 1726 stating that the framework inside was then removed as it was decayed. At the far end of the main avenue is an animal cemetery with inscribed stones built into the wall. The pool and fine Norman church are well worth a visit, as is the old tithe barn at the west door.

97 Cruck House   E9

One of the earliest methods of house building was to split curved tree trunks down their lengths and rear them tent-fashion to a ridge beam. Cross members held them rigid and wattle and daub were used to fill in between. This simple idea was introduced about the fourteenth century and continued to the eighteenth, long after more elaborate methods had been introduced. The eighteenth century saw wattle and daub replaced by bricks, as in this example at Melbourne, beside the B587 Staunton Harold road. Close by are a group of almshouses and a chapel built and endowed by Thomas Cook, founder of the world famous travel agency. He was born in a cottage in Quick Close nearby, which has recently been demolished.

Anchor Church E9

The burial of 'Ye fool at Anchor Church' is recorded at Repton Church in 1658, so this cave beside a quiet backwater of the River Trent near Ingleby has been known by that name for at least 300 years. A terrible legend of the twelfth century seems to date it even earlier when Sir Hugo de Burdett lived with his young wife at Knowle Hills not far away. A distant relative named Baron of Boyvill of Castleton desired the wife Johanne and contrived a plot with a travelling friar named Bernard. Sir Hugo was persuaded by Bernard that his duty lay with the Crusaders, and soon the Baron arrived at Knowle Hills with the news that Sir Hugo had been killed in the Holy Land and the estate was his. Grief stricken, Johanne repulsed him, but the marriage was arranged when suddenly, on the eve of the wedding, Sir Hugo returned. Overjoyed, Johanne ran to meet him with outstretched arms, but Sir Hugo drew his sword and she lay in the courtyard with a severed hand. The knight had slain the Baron in the woods after being taunted of his wife's unfaithfulness. There the story might have ended, but one day the lonely Sir Hugo received a message entreating him to go to Anchor Church, where a dying monk begged his forgiveness. The whole plot was revealed, for the monk was Bernard who was ending his days in penitence there. Black Pool is a portion of the old river course which carved the cliff from the soft sandstone. The cave may have been natural, but has been enlarged into two rooms with windows. Today Anchor Church and its Black Pool are the haunt of fishermen and the occasional heron. It is shown on the 1 inch ordnance map and can be reached by a footpath from Ingleby, or from the road opposite Foremark Hall, long the home of the Burdetts and now a school.

99 Lud's Church A5

In dramatic contrast to Anchor Church in its pastoral setting, is Lud's Church on the Staffordshire-Cheshire border near Wincle. Lud's Church is a deep rocky cleft in Forest Wood on the steep slopes of Back Forest in the Dane Valley. Here in this gloomy chasm where the sun never shines met the Lollards, it is said, one of the first opposition movements leading to the Reformation. Under constant persecution, they met in secret. The name Lud's Church is believed to come from the fifteenth century when a Walter de Ludauk, a zealous follower of the movement, met here with friends and was captured in a skirmish. Legend has it that his granddaughter was killed and is buried close by the entrance to the cave. The defile was no doubt caused by a landslip opening a fault in the rock, and extends about 200ft into the hillside, is about 50ft deep and about 9ft wide, with steep stone steps leading down into the damp gloom. For many years a white figurehead made of wood stood high on the rocky walls, but it was smashed some years ago. This was known as 'Lady Lud' but had no connection with the place, being a figurehead from the ship *Swythamley*. Swythamley Hall lies about one mile southwest of Lud's Church. Lud's Church is shown on the 1 inch ordnance map near Gradbach, about 3 miles south of Flash.

100 Eyam's Saxon Cross C3

The wonderful cross in Eyam churchyard dates from the ninth century, when itinerant Christian missionaries arrived from the north to establish the new faith. The Madonna, Angels and Christ in Glory can be discerned and the original, 10ft high, would have been a splendid thing. Unfortunately 2ft of the shaft is missing, and it is recorded that it was 'knocked to pieces for domestic purposes'. Thought to have been found on the moors, the cross lay in a corner of the churchyard in the eighteenth century, and today it stands as the pride of Eyam and the only one in the Midlands with its head complete. The sundial (Plate 53) is close by and Plate 20 briefly tells the story of the plague here.

101 Cross, Stile, Cross   C6

Of the same date as the one at Eyam the cross at Bradbourne has suffered sadly, its curious smoothness in places calling for explanation. As can be seen, the top portion has been split and the carving worn away. This has been caused by countless boots and trouser legs, for until it was rescued and rebuilt the two top portions had been used as a typical V-stile into the churchyard. Not far away stands a much newer cross over the grave of Nat Gould, a native of Derbyshire and author of popular racing novels in the early part of this century.

102 Fine Wayside Cross   B3

There are a number of ancient wayside crosses in the Peak District, perhaps set up by religious houses to guide travellers across the featureless moors. They are usually located on a prominent point, or at the crossing of tracks as at Edale Cross on the Edale to Hayfield route, and Hollins Cross on the Mam Tor-Win Hill ridge, both shown on the 1 inch ordnance map. All these require some walking, but the finest example is easily found at Wheston near Tideswell, beside the road. Dating from the fifteenth century, it has the Crucifixion carved on one side, and the Madonna and Child on the other, and is over 11ft high.

103 Lost Market Town D4

Leash Fen is a wet area of moorland about six miles north-west of Chesterfield, but it seems it was not always so. Evidence of building has been found here, and the five or six worn crosses around the fen may have been boundary stones. One of these is Whibbersley Cross, which is shown on the 1 inch ordnance map near Clod Hall, beside the Curbur to Chesterfield road. Some credence is given to the legend of a lost town by an ancient rhyme which reads:
*When Chesterfield was heath and broom,
Leash Fen was a market town,
Now Leash Fen is all heath and broom
And Chesterfield a market town.*

104 Lion's Head Rock C6

This remarkable likeness to a lion's head is probably the most famous of the Peak's natural curiosities. Situated in Dovedale, this limestone cliff is about 1½ miles upstream from the Stepping Stones, and the best view is looking back downstream. Another 1½ miles brings one to Viator's Bridge (Plate 13) and the road in Milldale, passing Ilam Rock, Dove Holes and Raven's Tor. Fittingly, here in the heart of this beautiful region, a plaque set in the rock below Lion's Head Rock records our debt to a man who did so much to preserve this area for all time. It reads, 'This dale and adjoining lands were acquired by the National Trust through the vision of the late F.A.Holmes, MA, JP of Buxton who worked to that end from 1916 to 1947'. Sir Robert McDougall was a great benefactor to the Peak District through the National Trust, and Mr Holmes told me a few years before he died how he had taken Sir Robert over the hills towards Dovedale. Blindfolded, Sir Robert was led onto Lover's Leap, a point high above the dale. The blindfold was removed and the breathtaking grandeur of the deep gorge revealed. When told it could be bought for preservation by the National Trust, Sir Robert replied, 'It's yours'. In November 1946, only two months before he died, Mr Holmes gave the conical hill of

High Wheeldon in the upper Dove Valley to the National Trust, in memory of the men of Derbyshire and Staffordshire who fell in World War II.

105 Fenny Bentley Hall   C6

With the appearance of 'half church, half hall' the old hall at Fenny Bentley attracts attention as one passes through the village on the A515 Ashbourne to Buxton road. The tower is all that remains from the fifteenth-century fortified and moated manor of the Beresfords.

06 The Beresford Tomb   C6

Thomas Beresford fought at Agincourt. Father of twenty-one children, he and his family are represented in Fenny Bentley church in a very weird way. Thomas and his wife Agnes are shown on a table tomb tied up in shrouds, while round the sides are their twenty-one children, also shrouded. Agnes died in 1463 and Thomas in 1473, and it is thought the tomb was erected about a century later and the sculptor had no portraits to guide him. Also notable in the church is a fine wooden rood screen, which according to a local legend was given by Thomas Beresford as a thanks offering after the Wars of the Roses.

107 Unfinished Millstones D3

Abandoned millstones are among the most interesting features of the Peak District, and this batch of several hundred lies below Surprise View, where the A625 Sheffield to Hathersage road cuts through Millstone Edge above the Derwent Valley. For perhaps two centuries they have waited for transport which has never come. On the moors above and in the quarries below we find them in various stages of manufacture, from the first chisel cut on a rough block of stone to the finished stone complete with hole. We may picture these lonely places alive with groups of men engaged in an industry which made Peak millstones and grindstones famous all over the world. All this seems to have ended as though the workers disappeared overnight, but in fact the cause was economic. The importation of French millstones in the mid eighteenth century which were claimed to be superior, spelled the end. But the industry did not die without a fight, for as local stones were replaced by foreign ones the enraged workers attacked the mills, destroying stones as far south as Derby, where it was necessary to read the Riot Act and restore order with military help from Nottingham. This now dead industry extended from over the Yorkshire border and down the Derwent Valley as far as Duffield, following the massive outcrops of Millstone Grit which form those dark 'edges' so typical of the Peak District. Old documents refer to a 'brussen' millstone on the hill above Shining Cliff Wood at Ambergate, and this broken stone is still there.

108 Trough on the Moors D3

Upon the moors above Millstone Edge can be found other evidence of the stonecutter's art, including a large stone trough abandoned in the process of being cut. The method of cutting is clearly seen, the shaping of the block and then the chiselling of a channel leaving the outer rim, the 'island' in the middle being hacked out later.

This particular example is cracked, this perhaps being the reason for its being abandoned. These troughs are found in use all over the Peak, and no doubt they were also in demand together with grindstones in the steel works of Sheffield not many miles away. The trough can be found among the heather not far from Toad's Mouth Rock.

109 Toad's Mouth Rock D3

This curious block of gritstone towers above the A625 road where it crosses Burbage Brook on the Derbyshire-Yorkshire border. It is easy to see how it got its name, although only the eye is artificial, an embellishment first noticed in a print in 1880. There is a small car park beside the road east of Toad's Mouth Rock, and a rough road leads up the valley to the trough shown above. Across the moors can be seen Carl Wark.

110 Carl Wark D2

This impressive hill-fort stands 1,200ft above sea level on the slopes of Higger Tor above Hathersage, and can be clearly seen from the road which passes Toad's Mouth Rock. A natural plateau of about two acres is fortified by a stone wall about 100ft long and nearly 10ft high, formed by huge blocks of millstone grit and strengthened by an earth ramp. The natural cliff on two other sides is reinforced by stones to make a formidable fortress, with an entrance to the south west. Its age is undecided, some experts thinking it dates from the Dark Ages immediately after the Roman occupation, but many now consider it to be an Iron Age hill-fort contemporary with those on Mam Tor and Fin Cop above Monsal Dale. Unlike these and others in the county, however, it is not connected with any known prehistoric trackway. Whatever its history, it gives a good reason for a very pleasant walk along well-worn paths through the heather, and a climb on the top of Higger Tor with its curiously weathered masses of stone is rewarding.

111 Blue John Mine   B2

This small unimposing building stands at the entrance to the famous Blue John Mine near Castleton. This blue flourspar is found only in the hill called Treak Cliff, situated between the Winnats and Mam Tor, and ornaments made from it have found their way all over the world. The brittle nature of fluorspar makes it difficult to fashion into large pieces, but visitors to Chatsworth House, however can see a huge vase made from Blue John, and Kedleston Hall has two chimneypieces inlaid with it. Today only small pieces are used in brooches etc. Visitors to the cave can see small deposits of the spar in the three miles of caves and caverns in the heart of Treak Cliff, which may also be entered in Treak Cliff Cavern not far away on the Castleton side of the hill.

112 Snake Pass   B1

One of the most exhilarating runs in the Peak takes one over the sinuous Snake Pass between Glossop and the Ladybower Reservoir. The name does not come from the twisting route, but from the Snake Inn about half way up the eastern side. The date 1821 over the doorway denotes when it was built as Lady Clough House, but later it became the Snake Inn, a snake featuring in the coat of arms of the Cavendish family. The road was built by Thomas Telford in 1821, and was the last of the great turnpike roads built in the Peak District.

113 Peak Cavern   C2

In the superstitious days of long ago the Devil was a very real person, and it is not surprising that he was thought to live in Peak Cavern at Castleton. Old prints show it as Devil's Hole from its former name of Peak's Arse or Devil's Arse, but whatever the origin, no cave anywhere could be a more desirable residence of Old Nick. The huge cavern, nearly 40ft high and 100ft wide, lies at the foot of the rocky chasm seen here, the cliffs rising 260ft. Here the sun never shines and the jackdaws reign as they have done for centuries. One of the seven wonders of the Peak, the cavern's passages extend at least 12,000ft into the hillside, linking several vast caverns with names like Orchestra Chamber, Bell House and Roger Rain House. These have been formed by water which has sunk into swallow holes on the hills above (Plate 80) and carved their way through the limestone to emerge at a lower level. Peak Water flows from the cavern to join the River Noe from Edale lower down the valley, but it is not surprising that coming from Devil's Hole it should also have once been called the River Styx.

114 Rope Making in Peak Cavern   C2

Over 400 years ago the floor of the entrance chamber of Peak Cavern, which extends 300ft into the hill, was terraced and rope making machinery installed. Several cottages were built inside, but these have now gone, although we can still see the rope walk standing exactly as it did when last used. The Marrison family of Castleton made ropes here for 200 years, and Mr Herbert Marrison was still making ropes in 1967 at the age of 83. Sash cords and ropes for breweries were made, also clothes lines, and a pretty custom was carried on of giving each Castleton bride a clothes line made in the cavern.

115 Peveril Castle C2

This view of Peveril Castle seen from Cave Dale, together with that of Peak Cavern, shows the almost impregnable position of this fortress, the only castle remains of any importance left in Derbyshire. The keep and the gateway, now in ruins, were built by Henry II in the twelfth century, but the castle originally dates from the eleventh century and was built by William Peveril, the Conqueror's bailiff for the area. There were other additions in later centuries, and the steep hill climb from Castleton is well worth while. It figures in fiction in Sir Walter Scott's *Peveril of the Peak*. Cave Dale is a limestone gorge entered from Castleton, and a footpath climbs about two miles to its head. From here one can return to Castleton by a rough road to the left via Dirtlow Rake, or to the right to the head of the Winnats and thence to Castleton, walks of about 3½ miles each.

116 Haunted Highlow Hall C3

Sixteenth-century Highlow Hall was once the home of the Archers, passing to the Eyres when the younger of two sisters married Nicholas Eyre, heir to the manor of Hope. Legend has it that the older sister was almost betrothed to Nicholas when she found he was also paying attention to her younger sister, and fled from the house for ever. Some time later her ghost glided down the great oak staircase to confront Nicholas and put a curse on the house of Eyre. Within the prescribed time this once great family was no more of note, but Highlow Hall remains. It stands beside the road which climbs steeply to Abney from Leadmill Bridge near Hathersage. Shown on the 1 inch ordnance survey map.

117 Hazlebadge Hall C3

Another grim legend of centuries ago is connected with this grey stone hall of 1549 standing in Bradwell Dale. Here lived the Vernon family, a member of which, Margaret, rode down the dale to Hope to see the man she loved married to someone else. Crazy with misery, she rode home to die, and on dark stormy nights her ghost gallops frenziedly through the rocky gorge to Hazlebadge Hall. The coat of arms of the Vernons together with that of the Swynnertons can be seen carved on the front of the hall. Shown on the 1 inch ordnance map.

118 Winnats B2

Grim and forbidding even today in the wintertime, the deep narrow gorge called the Winnats near Castleton was a place to be avoided centuries ago. Until the new road was built about 1817 round the foot of Mam Tor, the rough track, originally a saltway, which drops steeply down this windy pass (the name means 'windgates') was the main turnpike road through the Hope Valley. Here in 1758 a young couple were murdered while on their way to Peak Forest, a Derbyshire 'Gretna Green' where runaway marriages were performed, their bodies lying hidden in a cave for ten years. Many years later a lead miner confessed on his death bed, telling of four others who were involved and had already died. One had died insane, another killed by a fall of stone, a third committed suicide and the fourth had broken his neck in a fall in the Winnats. At the foot of the gorge lies Speedwell Mine, where we can see the saddle of the murdered girl. The mine is open to the public, and one may descend many steps and enjoy the unique experience of travelling by boat along the flooded lead mine to a great cavern called the Bottomless Pit.

119 Eagle Stone   D3

An interesting tale is told of Eagle Stone not far from Wellington's Monument (Plate 136) on Baslow Edge. Many years ago the young men of Baslow had to show their prowess and fitness for marriage by climbing this huge stone, and the fact that the village had its fair share of weddings is not due to its youth being a race of mountaineers, but to there being an easy way up. An easy but very exhilarating walk along Baslow Edge can be made from Curbar Gap above Curbar (Plate 38) visiting Eagle Stone, Wellington Monument and the moorland guidestone (Plate 137). It would take a whole book to show all the various rock formations in the Peak District, and by reason of their location on moors and edges, they are worth finding for their views alone. Salt Cellar, Wheel Stones and Cakes of Bread on Derwent Edge, Seal Stones on Seal Edge and Blackwoman's Stones on Blackden Edge are among a number shown on the 1 inch ordnance map.

120 Tiny Guard House   D4

This very small guard house stands on the bridge over the River Derwent at Baslow. Unlike Shardlow's Tollhouse (Plate 47) no record of toll charges exists, nor has it a name like Ha'penny Bridge at Ambergate which reminds us of the charge for pedestrians there. The only surviving record is a decree of 1500 as to what may not pass over the bridge: 'no one shall henceforth lead or carry any millstones over the bridge to Basselowe under pain of 6/8d'. Derbyshire has many old tollhouses still left on its turnpike roads, an octagonal example still standing in Stony Middleton, and another with a carving of a bell and a gate (tollgate) standing beside the Hassop to Great Longstone road, both only three or four miles from Baslow.

121 An Unusual Clock Face   D4

If you are one of those people who always glance at church tower clock faces, you will have a surprise at Baslow, for the word *Victoria* and the date 1897 have been used in place of the numerals. This was done to commemorate the Queen's Diamond Jubilee and it was fortunate that there were just the right number of letters and numerals. It was the idea of Dr E.M. Welch of Baslow whose name we see on Wellington's Monument (Plate 136), and who did much to instil pride of country in the young folk of the district. There is a stained glass window to his memory in the church.

122 Dog Whips in Church   D4

The thought of using a whip to chase stray dogs from church during a service raises a smile, yet this was once a common practice. The Youlgreave church wardens' accounts for several hundred years included the salary of the dog-whipper 'for whipping ye dogges forthe of ye churche in tyme of divyne service', Herbert Walton receiving sixteen pence for the duty in 1609. It is perhaps not surprising that almost all these whips have disappeared from our churches, and only one may still be seen in the county, preserved in a glass case at Baslow. Sometimes the dog-whipper's duty included keeping the congregation in order, and at Castleton in 1722 ten shillings was paid to the 'sluggard-waker' who used a long wand to tap anyone who looked like dozing off.

The other object is a pitch-pipe used in 1856 for re-tuning the organ.

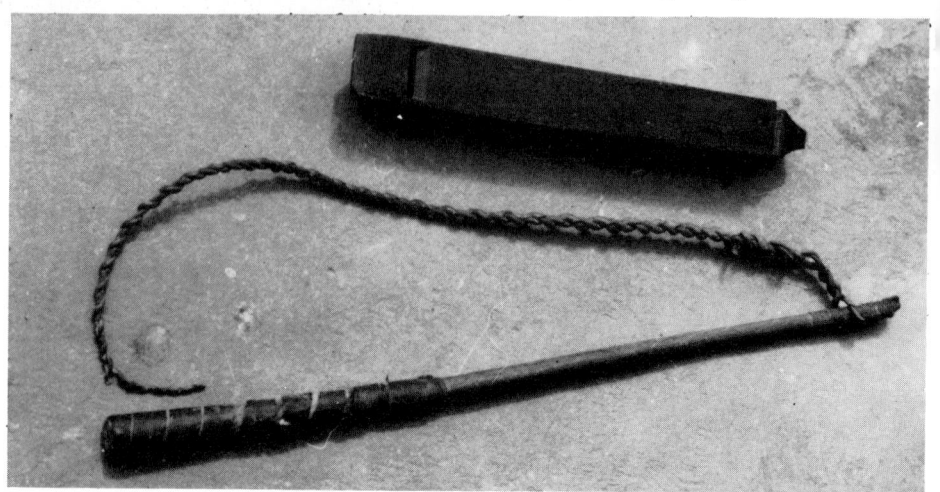

123 Bess of Hardwick's Monument
E8

Often the proud Bess of Hardwick would visit All Saints' Church in Derby and look at this pretentious alabaster monument which she had designed for herself. Elizabeth Hardwick was born at Hardwick Hall south of Chesterfield in 1518. She married at 14, was widowed at 15, and when she died in 1608 had outlived three more husbands. She amassed enormous wealth, two of the marriages being into the Cavendish family and the Earls of Shrewsbury. In 1549 she bought Chatsworth for £600 and replaced it with a splendid new house of which little remains today. Her last marriage was to the Sixth Earl of Shrewsbury who was for many years troubled with the custody of Mary Queen of Scots (Plate 3). So ambitious had Bess become, she tried to link herself with royalty by marrying a Cavendish daughter to Mary Queen of Scot's brother-in-law, who was in possible line with both the English and Scottish thrones. Queen Elizabeth was 'not amused' and Bess served a sentence in The Tower. At the time of his marriage the Earl was said to be the richest man in England, but he died broken in spirit and destitute, too poor to find an executor. The old hall where Bess was born stands in ruins not far from the last of the great houses she built. Hardwick Hall, 'more glass than wall', is a finer monument to the termagent Bess than this one in the county town.

124 Dorothy Vernon's Monument
C4

'By the grace of God I am what I am', reads the pathetic inscription over the effigy of a child on the monument of Sir George Manners in Bakewell Church, for the child was weak minded. The monument which visitors come to see, however, is that of Sir George's parents, Dorothy Vernon and Sir John Manners who were said to have eloped so romantically from Haddon Hall so long ago. True or false, this tale has gripped the imagination for over 400 years, and caused many people to come from far and near to gaze on this monument. These monuments are in the Vernon Chapel where there are two tomb chests to the Vernons, both with alabaster effigies, one showing Sir George of 1567 with his two wives. The church has a most unusual fourteenth century monument to Sir Godfrey Foljambe and his wife, a fourteenth-century font, and an amazing number of fragments of Saxon carvings in the porch. In the churchyard stands the shafts of two Saxon crosses, one of which was unearthed in a field above Darley Dale.

125 Swarkestone Bridge   E9

According to popular legend, Swarkestone Bridge which is nearly a mile long and has seventeen arches, was built in the thirteenth century at the expense of two sisters who saw their lovers drowned while trying to cross the flooded meadows. At the southern end shown here one may see beneath the arches the original packhorse bridge width, from the days when this was the main crossing of the Trent in the Midlands. As such it was of great strategic importance, Bonnie Prince Charlie sent on his soldiers to establish a bridgehead here before his retreat from Derby in 1745. At the northern end where the bridge crosses the river, can be found the foundations of a bridge chapel. Undulating and twisting across the valley, this raised causeway is unable to cope with modern traffic, and a move is afoot to widen or bypass it. Shown on the 1 inch ordnance map, it is classified as an ancient monument.

126 An Uncrowned King   F9

Thought to be unique in England, the carved stone below the village cross at King's Newton records the ascent to the throne on 20 January 1936 of Edward, Prince of Wales. For 325 days he reigned as King Edward VIII but was never crowned, abdicating on 10 December to be succeeded by his brother George VI.

127 Balcony Field E9

The purpose for which the Balcony Field at Swarkestone was built is a matter for conjecture. The Stuart or Jacobean building at the far end looks onto a walled enclosure about 100yd long by 60yd wide called The Cuttle, and some historians believe that bull-baiting was practiced here. Others think that the Grandstand, as the building is also called, was used to watch nothing more harmless than bowls, although it has also been suggested that jousting took place here. There are even those who claim it as the Tournament Field in Ivanhoe, but Smisby a little further south will have none of this, for they claim the site quite near their village. Little remains of the home of the Harpurs with which the Balcony Field was connected, but Swarkestone Church, situated in the corner of the field, has some alabaster tombs to the family in the Harpur Chapel. One can walk past the church down to the river to continue along the bank to Swarkestone Bridge.

128 Early Iron Furnaces E6

These curious stone structures stand in open fields close to and on the west side of the Ripley bypass, about one mile south of Ripley, in an area known as Morley Park. They are very intersting relics of the earliest of those methods of smelting iron which used coke, and were built by Francis Hurt of Alderwasley Hall in the late eighteenth and early nineteenth centuries. Alternate charges of coke, iron ore and limestone were loaded into the top from the hillside, and the molten metal run off at the bottom to form pig iron. The furnaces could be run continuously for three years, the glow in the sky being visible from Alderwasley in the Derwent Valley, no doubt giving great satisfaction to Francis Hurt. About 35ft high and once surmounted by cupolas, these old buildings are interesting survivals of an early industrial advance, and today are preserved as ancient monuments.

129 Crich Stand E6

Flashing at intervals like a lighthouse in the night, Crich Stand, high on its quarry edge above the Derwent Valley south of Matlock, can be seen in five counties. This is at least the third tower to stand on this spot, for the previous two, one of 1788 built by Francis Hurt of Alderwasley Hall and another of 1851 were both damaged by lightning. In 1923 the present tower was opened as a memorial to the men of the Sherwood Foresters who fell in World War I and now it also commemorates those who died in World War II. In the quarry below is situated the Crich Tramway Museum, fronted by the imposing facade of the old Assembly Rooms from the Market Place in Derby.

130 Tower on the Chevin E7

Not far from Crich Stand (above) this simple structure on the Chevin above Milford, a little further down the Derwent Valley, is a long way from it in spirit and purpose. Its origin is obscure until one notices the round ventilation shaft close by, indicating that we are directly over a railway tunnel. When the railway was being constructed in 1839 this look-out tower was built as a liaison between the two gangs of men cutting the tunnel from both sides of the hill. Inside can be seen the remains of four floors, the top two having fireplaces, and a huge stone base almost filling the ground floor. Here, it is suggested, stood machinery used in digging the ventilation shaft. A steep road climbs from Milford to the tower, and here it becomes a rough green track along the ridge of the Chevin to the road above Farnah Green, a very pleasant walk.

31 Peter's Stone   C3

Standing in a dry dale between Tideswell and Wardlow, this curious circular mass of limestone capped by a dome of grass-covered soil, is shown on the 1 inch ordnance map as Peter's Stone. Perhaps the name came from a likeness to St Peter's in Rome. The dale becomes a deep wooded gorge and two miles away the stream it has gathered joins the Wye at Cressbrook Mill. A footpath passing through the mill-yard continues beside the Wye through Water-cum-Jolly, to emerge into Millers Dale through the yard of Litton Mill a little over a mile away, an easy walk through a lovely limestone dale.

32 Little St Paul's   C7

Although dedicated to St Mary, 'Little St Paul's' is the popular name given to this tiny church at Mapleton in the Dove Valley about two miles north of Ashbourne. Erected in the eighteenth century, it replaced one built in the fifteenth of which no stone remains. Just beside the bridge over the river nearby a stile indicates a footpath upstream which passes Coldwall Bridge (Plate 66), and continues into Dovedale. Over the bridge in Staffordshire stands Okeover Hall with fine wrought-iron gates by Robert Bakewell.

133 Parson's Tor C4

This limestone crag towering high over the upper reaches of Lathkill Dale is called Parson's Tor. Known as Fox Tor until 1776, it was then renamed after the Rector of Monyash, the Rev Thomas Lomas, who, returning from Bakewell one stormy night, fell headlong from its edge into the valley below. The following morning his ghost was seen in the village, and a search revealed the dead man at the foot of the crag. He lies in the churchyard at Monyash. In the dale below is a cave from which the River Lathkill flows in wet weather, but in times of drought the water rises from the river bed lower down the valley. A footpath runs the whole length of Lathkill dale from near Monyash to Alport Village. It starts about half a mile from Monyash on the B5055 road to Bakewell where the road dips into the shallow head of the dale. Here we may turn through a gate on the right to drop down an open field and enter the upper reaches of the gorge which are of bare limestone, the lower reaches being pleasantly wooded. The tor and cave lie about half a mile down the dale and Alport about 5 miles. There are remains of extensive lead mining in the dale.

134 Nelson's Monument D4

Derbyshire had its Nelson's Column only five years after Waterloo, while Londoners had to wait a further thirty for theirs! It stands 12ft high on rocky Birchin Edge overlooking Baslow in the Derwent Valley, 1,000ft above sea level. A simple gritstone obelisk, it was erected in 1810 by John Brightman, a Baslow man.

35 Victory, Defiant and Royal Soverin   D4

Near to Nelson's Monument are three huge rocks looking somewhat like ships with the names *Victory*, *Defiani* and *Royal Soverin* (sic) carved on their bows. The monument and rocks can clearly be seen about 1½ miles from Baslow on the Chesterfield road, and can be reached on foot from beside the Robin Hood Inn. For centuries this track was shunned, for in Saxon times it was known as Wormshill or Dragon's Den, a place to be avoided in those days.

36 Wellington's Monument   D3

Clearly seen by travellers on the A621 Baslow-Sheffield road where it climbs from the Derwent Valley, this 10ft-high cross stands on Baslow Edge, 1,000ft above sea level. It bears the inscription 'Wellington, Born 1769 Died 1852. Erected 1866 by E.M.Wrench, late 34th Reg'mt'.

Although presumably built to balance Nelson's Monument on Birchin Edge, several guide books including J.B.Firth's excellent *Highways and Byways of Derbyshire* state that it was built to commemorate the visit of the Iron Duke as the guest of the Duke of Rutland, but there seems no positive record of this.

137 Moorland Guidestone   D3

Centuries ago the Peak District was avoided whenever possible. The wild lonely moors had their rough tracks, still discernible together with guidestones bearing the name of the next town. Set up voluntarily until an act of 1702 made them compulsory at track junctions, they would be a very welcome sight on the skyline. We may take this as an early example, as later the mileage was inscribed. It is interesting to look for guidestones, perhaps serving as gateposts, and often the old spelling is given.

138 England's Second Oldest Font?   F8

Wilne church stands strangely isolated in the flat meadows near the confluence of the Trent and Derwent. Gradually through the years the people have deserted this spot owing to flooding, with only a few cottages now left standing and deserted. The church is the proud possessor of an ancient font with Saxon carvings from the seventh or eighth century, claimed by some experts as the second oldest in the country. It is firmly believed that it was not originally a font, but is in fact a portion of a huge round cross, inverted and hollowed out. In 1916 a fire swept through the church, and as can be seen, some of the carving has flaked off.

139 Stones from the Sea   F9

This fine lychgate stands at Aston-on-Trent church, and is a memorial to James Holden, a Rector here for 50 years. Carved oak timbers catch the eye, but the curious feature is the grey stones of its roof, said to have been brought from the sea. Aston church has an unusual link with Shardlow, for after the opening of the Trent and Mersey Canal the population there greatly increased, and they had no church of their own. A 'church boat' took Shardlow worshippers to Aston every Sunday morning, the south aisle being set aside for them. Perhaps this direct link with the sea has some connection with the lychgate roof.

140 Remarkable Coffin Lid D6

This wonderful panel of carvings showing scenes from the life of Christ is a proud possession of Wirksworth Church. Although now built into an interior wall, it was originally the cover of a sarcophogus dating from about 800AD. It measures approximately 5ft by 3ft and there are forty figures, but it is incomplete, for the Cross would almost certainly be central.

Perhaps the finest example of early Christian carving in Derbyshire, it was found in 1820 upside down over a vault near the altar, a position which no doubt helped maintain its fine condition. Other fragments of ancient carving are built into the walls, one in the south transept depicting a lead miner with his tools, a reminder that not far from the north gate of the churchyard is the Moot Hall in Chapel Lane (Plate 73).

141 Joseph Sowter's Second Wife E7

A strange domestic story is told of this tombstone in Duffield Churchyard. It was erected by Joseph Sowter to his wife Elizabeth in 1794, and on remarrying he very unwisely continually extolled the virtues of his first wife to the second. Inevitably the breaking point arrived, with his new wife storming off with a blunderbuss to fire at the tombstone. Here the essence of the story may be in doubt, for the resultant holes are in that half of the stone left vacant for the husband's name. Perhaps her aim was not so inaccurate!

Norbury Tombchests B7

Derbyshire has many fine examples of alabaster work, and Norbury is justly proud of her possessions. Here are the tombs of the Fitzherberts, the remains of their thirteenth-century hall still standing near the church. There are two similar tombchests, one to Sir Nicholas and his wife with their seventeen children, and the other to Sir Ralph and his wife with fifteen children. All the children are carved in relief standing beneath arches around the sides of the tomb. Of particular interest is the small figure of a lion upon which Sir Ralph's feet rest, with a tiny monk perched upon the lion's back. Standing high above the River Dove, Norbury church is one of the best in Derbyshire and well worth a visit.

Almost certainly the alabaster in Norbury church came from Chellaston near Derby, for in the Middle Ages the quarries there sent large quantities all over England and the continent. Many of our tombs and monuments were carved at Nottingham, and large unfashioned blocks were shipped down the Trent for abroad. Today the deposits at Chellaston are almost worked out.

143 A Wonderful Lectern E8

One of the most unusual objects made from alabaster is this wonderful lectern in Mackworth church, made in 1903 and carved from a single block of stone. Delicate and looking translucent in certain lights, it represents grape vines twining round a column with their roots forming the base, with leaves and grapes beneath the Bible support. It may well be unique.

144 Unusual Norman Font C5

Unlike the soft alabaster seen above, gritstone does not lend itself to delicate carving. This coarser material was used for the twelfth-century font in Youlgreave church, and has the unusual feature of a small water stoup carved on the side and apparently held in the mouth of a dragon-like creature. This is a rare treasure, and really belongs to the neighbouring village of Elton, for in 1838 it was thrown into the churchyard there to find its way into a garden in Youlgreave and then into the church. Eventually Elton came to realise its loss and now has to be satisfied with a copy.

145 Derbyshire's Canal Pioneer   B3

It is strange that the Peak District, where canals are practically impossible, should have produced James Brindley, great civil engineer and pioneer of the canal system of this country. At Wormhill near Tideswell, stands a fountain in his memory, a tablet reading 'In memory of James Brindley, Civil Engineer, Born in this Parish AD 1716', while a small stone with a bronze plaque indicates the site of his birthplace not far away at Tunstead. This was erected by the Derbyshire Archaeological Society and says of Brindley: 'Of humble birth, he became famous as the pioneer builder of the great canals of this country'.

The Trent and Mersey Canal together with its branch the Caldon Canal, which runs close to the Peak District, and the Chesterfield Canal, are his work, although he did not live to see them completed. He also devised and built much mill machinery, and Brindley Mill at Leek has been restored and is open to the public at specific times.

146 Ironwater Spring   E8

Quorndon's hopes of becoming a spa were suddenly ended when an earthquake stopped its mineral spring in 1896. An ironwater spring, together with a sulphur spring in Kedleston Park, had raised the village's hopes, for the waters were already being sold in Derby, and a hotel had been built for patients near Kedleston. This still stands, and after many years as Bath Farm it is now a hotel again. The village spring, which is well maintained and stands beside the road which climbs to Quorndon church, still drips slowly into a trough. The mineral waters of Quorndon or Quorn were noted by Daniel Defoe in his tour of Great Britain, so it seems that this well is at least 250 years old.

147 Mermaid's Pool A5

The lonely moors of Morridge north-east of Leek rise to 1,600ft above the sea at Merryton Low, and not far away is Blakemere, often called Mermaid's Pool. Here, tradition has it, lives a mermaid in a bottomless pool, and should you be so foolish to be in this bleak spot at the unearthly hour of midnight you deserve your fate. This you may read in the old drover's inn called the Mermaid not far away, for there it is recorded that 'She calls on you to greet her, combing her dripping crown, And if you go to meet her, she ups and drags you down'. Across the valley seen behind is the Roaches where there is a similar pool called Doxy Pool, and there is another Mermaid's Pool below Kinder Downfall on Kinder Scout.

148 Winking Eye A5

The A53 Leek to Buxton road climbs steeply past Ramshaw Rocks at the eastern end of the Roaches, and travellers from Leek often have a surprise here. At one point an outcrop of rock has a remarkable likeness to a face, complete with a hole for an eye. What is astonishing, however, is that as one moves on the eye appears to close and open in a wink, an effect caused by another rock passing behind the eye to shut out the sky for a brief moment. Not even Lion's Head Rock (Plate 104) or Toad's Mouth Rock (Plate 109) can boast such realism!

149 Lost Village C2

Beneath the waters of the Ladybower Reservoir lies the site of the village of Derwent Woodlands. Here stood Derwent Hall, church and cottages, a delightful spot which was flooded when the dam was completed in 1945. Here too stood the packhorse bridge shown opposite. For some years the church tower was left standing, rising from the waters to show where the village once stood, but it was later demolished as unsafe, for in time of drought it was entered by visitors. At such times one can enjoy the rare experience of walking the streets of the village, although no buildings now remain. Today all that can be seen is the village war memorial, re-erected beside the new road on the hillside overlooking the spot where the village once stood.

150 Devotion of Tip C1

This tablet to Tip the sheepdog stands on the roadside close by the dam wall of Derwent Reservoir. The devotion of Tip is briefly told on the stone, of how in the winter of 1953/4 she kept watch beside her dead master in the deep snow on Howden Moor for fifteen weeks. Her emaciated body was nursed back to health, to be presented with a bronze medal, and even feature in a well-dressing scene. But her ordeal had been too great, for she died a year later on 16 February 1955, and she was buried on the moors where she had kept faithful vigil. This memorial was erected by subscriptions from all over the world.

151 Derwent Packhorse Bridge   C1

This seventeenth-century packhorse bridge now spans the Derwent near it source on the lonely moors above the Howden Reservoir. Originally it stood in the village of Derwent Woodlands, and when the Ladybower Reservoir was being built the bridge was photographed and each stone numbered before being carefully taken down and stored for the duration of World War II. After the war it was re-erected on its present site as a memorial to John Derry, a Sheffield lover of these hills, and the Sheffield Branch of the CPRE raised funds to this end. It was opened in 1959. A stone in the centre of the downstream parapet once held a cross, and it is believed that the bridge was built in the village by the White Canons of Welbeck just over the border in Nottinghamshire. They had great estates hereabouts with four chapels and two granges. To find the bridge pass the Ladybower, Derwent and Howden Reservoirs and continue to the end of the road (parking space). Here cross a footbridge to continue along a rough track for about half a mile to the bridge at Slippery Stones, a fitting spot for here it stands on the same packhorse track it served in the village, although this was originally a ford. Across the river is Yorkshire.

152 Well Dressing C3

The decoration of our wells and springs with flowers is one of our most delightful customs, and although one or two other counties practice well-dressing, Derbyshire excels. Whether the custom originated at Tissington whose springs never ran dry during a great drought in 1615, or began even earlier in the fourteenth century when not a soul was lost during the Black Death, is uncertain. The earliest records of Tissington dressing its wells are of about 250 years ago, and about 150 years ago they began the present method of well-dressing with elaborate and intricate scenes mounted on large wooden frames. A layer of soft clay is pressed onto the frame and the scene pricked out. Flower petals, berries and evergreens together with bark, lichen and small pieces of glittering flourspar and even wood are pressed into the clay, their vivid colours and textures making a scene of amazing realism. Words or pictures cannot do justice to their beauty, but they should be seen within a few days of completion to see them at their best. At Tissington a service is held in the church after Ascension Day when all five wells are visited and blessed. Until 1977 the scenes were mostly Biblical, but in that year, the Jubilee of Queen Elizabeth II was the theme of several of the twenty or so villages which now dress their wells or taps. For many years Tideswell has produced a superb picture of a cathedral over the well in the market place, accurate perspective giving depth and realism as seen here.

153 Shrovetide Football C7

Derbyshire is often described as a county of contrasts, and so it is with her customs when one compares the well dressing shown opposite with what passes for football at Ashbourne on Shrove Tuesday and Ash Wednesday. Here on a pitch 3 miles long and no definite width, with two watermills on the Henmore Brook as goals, a free-for-all Rugby type of football takes place. As one can imagine, a lot of the play takes place in the brook. The two sides are composed of those born north of the brook, the Up'ards, and those born south, the Down'ards, there being no limit to the number. A gaily painted ball is thrown up by a local or national celebrity, and a score is made by touching the water-wheel of the mills with it, the scorer being allowed to keep the ball and another one thrown up. The rules other than this are non-existent, but after a fine run down the wing by a car, the use of vehicles is now ruled out. Nothing certain is known of the game's origin, but it was played in many places all over England. No doubt it was a change from cock-fighting and bull-baiting, and there was always the chance of settling old scores. In Derby in 1796 a man was drowned in the Derwent while taking part, and efforts to stop it were not successful until 50 years later. Derbyshire has a number of other old customs, and while the rough and tumble of football is going on at Ashbourne, Winster is enjoying its pancake races. Garland Day takes place at Castleton on Oakapple Day, there is Church Clipping at Wirksworth and Burbage, Morris Dancing is having a revival and the Curfew is still rung in one or two villages.

154 The River Manifold Disappears B6

A caprice of the River Manifold not shared by its more famous companion the Dove, is its disappearance below ground in dry weather. Just below Wetton Mill, at Darfur Crags about halfway between the two bridges, the river sinks into its bed, although if there is a surplus of water this continues to other 'sinks' a little further downstream. At Beeston Tor about two miles downstream the Manifold is joined by the Hamps which also goes underground in times of drought.

155 The River Manifold Reappears B6

The waters of the Manifold and Hamps rivers reappear from beneath a small crag within a few yards of each other in the grounds of Ilam Hall. Although in wet weather they flow together above ground, below ground they take completely different courses before uniting here at Ilam. This has been proved by the use of corks, and the fact that the water temperatures are always several degrees different, although the famous Dr Johnson would not accept this when he was told of it on one of his visits to Ilam Hall where he had written *Rasselas*. Here behind the hall the Manifold leaves its valley by a great ampitheatre of woods in a spot known as Paradise.

156 Congreve's Grotto B6

Another literary link with Ilam is a small grotto above the cliff. Here is a table and bench of stone where the famous dramatist William Congreve wrote *The Old Batchelor* at the age of 18. The hall Congreve knew has gone, rebuilt last century by the Watts Russells, who also rebuilt the village and erected the village cross there. Today what is left of the hall is a Youth Hostel, and together with 50 acres is the property of the National Trust, the gift of Sir Robert McDougall.

157 St Bertram's Tomb B6

Long before the events above, St Bertram had chosen this lovely, secluded corner of Staffordshire as his home. His tomb lies within the church near the hall, and afflicted pilgrims used to come from afar to lie upon it in the hope of a cure. In contrast to this simple thirteenth-century relic is the full-size marble statue by Sir Francis Chantry, depicting a death-bed scene of David Watts with his daughter and her children. Also in the church are paper garlands hanging high in an arch, a relic of the old custom of carrying them at the funeral of a virgin; Matlock and Ashford-in-the-Water also have examples. The font is Saxon and the shafts of two Saxon crosses stand in the churchyard, while a third, uncovered in a cottage when the village was being rebuilt, stands beside the path in Paradise. Near the church is St Bertram's Well.

158 Thor's Cave   B6

Although the Manifold Valley in Staffordshire has never been aclaimed like its neighbour Dovedale, it has its own charm and character. But Dovedale has nothing to compare with Thor's Cave, dramatically situated high in Thor's Cliff which towers 350ft above the river where the road from Wetton Village drops steeply down to Wetton Mill in the valley. Although the name may have come from tor, it is more likely to be derived from Thor, the Norse God of thunder, while the name of the village of Wetton may come from the same source, for Thor was the son of the god Woden. The cave is 30ft high and 23ft wide with a huge pillar in the centre reaching to the roof, and a second pillar called the altar. Here the cave divides into two which extend into the hillside. The first serious excavation was made in 1864-5 by the Midland Scientific Association under the direction of Samuel Carrington of Wetton, and flint arrow-heads, bronze brooches, an iron adze and many other items were found, indicating some use of the cave from Romano-British to the present times. A complete skeleton thought to be Neolithic was found carefully buried in an upright position. Only 7ft of the clay floor was removed, and the cave has never been thoroughly excavated. There are a number of smaller caves in this area of the valley, and stories of ghosts and spirits are numerous. Perhaps the most popular is 'Fiddling Hobhurst' whose screeching on his fiddle in Thor's Cave years ago led to it being called Hob Hurst's House.

59 Railway in the Manifold Valley B6

Surprisingly even a railway wormed its way into the Manifold's rocky valley. In 1904 a narrow gauge branch line opened, forking from the North Staffordshire Railways at Waterhouses in the Hamps Valley to join the Manifold at Beeston Tor and continue to a terminus at Hulme End three miles from Hartington. It was hoped the railway would serve the farms and villages of the upper end of the valley, and revive the lead and copper mines once worked at Ecton (Plate 36). Its aims never materialised, for as one local sage said, 'It started nowhere and finished up in the same place', and in 1934 the Leek and Manifold Valley Light Railway closed. Today the route is owned by the Staffordshire County Council, and has been macadamed to make an easy and very scenic walk of about 8 miles. Motorists can use a portion of it from Swainsley Tunnel, seen here, to rejoin the road at Wetton Mill.

60 Manifold Dovecote B6

Not far from the tunnel stands Swainsley Hall, and many years ago the owner built a dovecote beside the river, one of the few built since they fell into disuse in the nineteenth century. The pigeons, however, deserted it for the farmbuildings, and today it serves as a charming fishing house. A closer look can be had from the old valley road between Swainsley and Wetton Mill, which is gated and not very suitable for vehicles.

Cottage Industry E6

Not far from the Market Place in Crich can be seen one of the few stockingers' houses still left in the county. Here, as in many thousands of homes in town and country in the eighteenth century, the whole family worked on stocking frames which were loaned out to them by a master hosier, who then bought the finished articles. Towards the end of the century conditions were bad, the owners issuing too many frames so that the workers had to undercut each other to make a living. In the early nineteenth century there were 4,000 frames in Derby alone, the workers and their families working 15 hours a day for a starvation living, conditions which led to rioting and machine breaking. The long windows conserved light and candles, and there are other examples of this cottage industry at Ockbrook and Cromford. In Duke Street in Derby a stockinger's house was demolished in recent years, and another awaiting demolition stands at the corner of Cheapside and Bold Lane.

62 Relic of a Silk Mill   A4

In contrast to the cottage industry were the large silk mills which followed John Lombe's success at Derby. Three silk mills were built in the tiny village of Wildboarclough about 7 miles south west of Buxton, and their size and importance is shown by the large administration block, which together with ruined buildings beside the Clough Brook, are all that remains of a once thriving industry. Perhaps this lonely village can lay claim to the largest sub Post Office in England, for that is what the building serves as today.

63 England's First Silk Mill   E8

Derbyshire and the Peak District is rich in industrial archaeology with its canals and railways, lead mining, iron founding, cotton and silk mills. Several areas where these activities took place are now being conserved, and in Derby what is usually considered England's first Silk Mill now fittingly houses Derby Industrial Museum. It was on an island in the Derwent that John Lombe built his factory in 1717, after surreptitiously obtaining the secrets of silk throwing from the Italians. Tradition has it that he was poisoned in revenge, but true or false, he died at the early age of 29, and was buried with a splendid funeral in All Saint's Church, now Derby Cathedral. The present building dates from 1910 when there was a disastrous fire, but it bears a fairly faithful resemblance to the original. It is hoped that the Silk Mill gates which now stand in Wardwick will be returned to their original site here.